Measurement of Poverty, Undernutrition and Child Mortality

T0326433

Göttinger Studien zur Entwicklungsökonomik
Göttingen Studies in Development Economics

Herausgegeben von/Edited by Hermann Sautter und/and Stephan Klasen

Bd./Vol. 24

PETER LANG

Frankfurt am Main · Berlin · Bern · Bruxelles · New York · Oxford · Wien

Mark Misselhorn

Measurement of Poverty, Undernutrition and Child Mortality

PETER LANG
Internationaler Verlag der Wissenschaften

Bibliographic Information published by the Deutsche Nationalbibliothek
The Deutsche Nationalbibliothek lists this publication in the Deutsche Nationalbibliografie; detailed bibliographic data is available in the internet at <http://www.d-nb.de>.

Zugl.: Göttingen, Univ., Diss., 2007

Cover illustration by courtesy of the
Ibero-Amerika-Institut für Wirtschaftsforschung, Göttingen.

D 7
ISSN 1439-3395
ISBN 978-3-631-57659-5

© Peter Lang GmbH
Internationaler Verlag der Wissenschaften
Frankfurt am Main 2008
All rights reserved.

Printed in Germany 1 2 3 4 5   7
www.peterlang.de

To Sabine

For all your support without which
I couldn't have accomplished this.

Editor's Preface

Although the world has seen a steady decline in poverty rates in the last two decades, the fight against poverty and inequality is far from over. The absolute number of persons living on less than $1 a day is still close to a billion persons. Especially when considering rising incomes elsewhere this high number of poor persons is increasingly unacceptable. Reducing poverty further, however, will require tough choices. This is especially the case when we take into account that poverty is not the only problem that has to be tackled in the coming decades. Considerable resources have to be devoted for example to the fight against communicable and non-communicable diseases like HIV/AIDS and Malaria or the fight against global warming.

It is therefore of fundamental importance to understand the determinants, and the most promising policies to fight poverty. But this requires agreement on the right indicators to monitor poverty in its many dimensions. Due to this multidimensionality of poverty there is a very large number of potential indicators and measurement issues are far from solved. This thesis contributes to the discussion of appropriate indicators for poverty measurement. All four essays are concerned with measurement issues of the different dimensions of poverty or are contributing to the literature on the determinants of poverty. In his first essay Mark Misselhorn focuses on studying the determinants of changes in income poverty at the macro level. The essay argues that the use of elasticities to measure changes in poverty rates over time is prone to misinterpretations and should therefore be avoided. These misinterpretations can be avoided by looking at absolute changes (i.e. percentage point changes) in headcount poverty, the poverty gap and the squared poverty gap. The paper also shows that this way one can better understand the respective roles of growth and distributional change on absolute poverty and predict the impact of both on future poverty reduction.

The second essay focuses on an especially important dimension of poverty, namely undernutrition. So far most multinational institutions measure changes in this dimension by looking at underweight, an anthropometric indicator that measures the weight of a child for a certain age and compares it to a reference standard. Due to the publication of a new reference standard that was published by the World Health Organization (WHO) in 2006 it is very likely that future progress will be measured using this new reference standard. In the essay it is argued that this opportunity should be used to not only switch to a new reference standard but also to a different indicator, namely stunting. The reason is that all weight-based anthropometric measures, such as underweight and wasting, suffer from the bias related to changes in the nutritional composition of diets in developing countries, which erroneously suggests falling rates of undernutrition that does not coincide with real improvements in the health of the affected children. This bias could lead to wrong conclusions concerning progress in the fight against undernutrition.

In the third essay, Mark Misselhorn examines the interdependencies and determinants of child mortality and child undernutrition in several countries in Sub-Saharan Africa and South Asia using representative microdata sets. In particular, he analyzes the question why child mortality is considerable higher in Africa than in South Asia although the incidence of child undernutrition is higher in South Asia than in Africa. He shows that differences in the determinants of both phenomena partly explain this puzzle. The overall poor health care system in African countries strongly contributes to the high rates of child mortality in this region whereas the relatively low nutritional status of mothers contributes to the high rates of child undernutrition in South Asia.

The last essay is concerned with the multidimensional measurement of poverty. Although there are a large number of different indicators, the probably best known measure is the Human Development Index (HDI). One of the most often heard critiques of the HDI is that is does not take into account inequality within countries in its three dimensions. In this essay a relatively easy and intuitive approach is suggested, which allows to compute the three components and the overall HDI for quintiles of the income distribution. This allows researchers and policy-makers to compare the level in human development of the poor with the level of the non-poor within countries, but also across countries.

These essays by Mark Misselhorn provide an extremely valuable contribution to the literature on the empirical analysis of poverty in its many dimensions.

Prof. Stephan Klasen, Ph.d.
Göttingen, December 2007

Author's Preface

It is well known that the road to the completion of a dissertation is stony and difficult to complete without the help of other persons. In my case special thanks of course go to Prof. Stephan Klasen. He can truly be called the 'Harry Potter of Science' because he has an answer to absolutely every question. He is by far the most educated person I have ever met. Besides without him I probably wouldn't have aspired a doctors degree. Several times I had the firm intent to leave Göttingen and return back home, but thanks to his persuasion and humaneness I always stayed. The enormous freedom he allowed me during the whole time was of tremendous importance for me. The offered trust hardly would have come from someone else.

I surely would have turned my back on Göttingen if I hadn't met my friends Dr. Ken "Ruban" Harttgen and Prof. Dr. Michael Grimm. Besides the nightly beers, the shared suffering as commuter to Munich, the uncompromising bodybuilding training, Michael was always willing and able to answer all scientific questions. Without the chaos control and permanent assistance by Ken I would have probably never finished my dissertation. It was of tremendous importance for me to have someone with whom I share so many views on so many things (okay, except on soccer!). In fact I would have never thought that I would make such a good friend in hostile territory, with whom I would start a very a promising Marathon and Triathlon career. Special thanks also go to Melanie and s'Güntherle, with whom I had numerous coffee breaks that kept the spirits high for all the research effort. Thanks also to all the other members of the Chair in Development Economics like Michaela, Johannes, Sebastian, Katharina, Denise and so on and so on, I really enjoyed working with you.

Very special thanks also go to Karl H. Wagner and Dr. Ulrich F. Geyer. Without the opportunity to earn some additional money during the whole time at university in Munich and Goettingen and without the continuous generosity I experienced by those two persons I would have met a lot more obstacles in the last years.

By far the largest burden had to be carried by my beloved girlfriend Sabine. To be forced to live together with someone who is never really there and never really away is no fun at all. Without her understanding and support I surely wouldn't have been able to write this dissertation. And even more important is that the road would have been stonier and a lot less beautiful than it actually was.

During all my steps up the ladder of our education system, my family was a continuous source of backing. Besides my brothers and sisters Hella, Dirk and Bettina, my parents were of decisive importance. Probably no one has ever had an easier and happier life than I have had so far. Therefore I want to use this seldom opportunity to say thank you to all of you.

Mark Misselhorn
Göttingen, Oktober 2007

Contents

List of Tables

List of Figures

Introduction and Overview

The State of Global Poverty

Over the past decades a mix of technology and economic integration transforming the world has lead to unprecedented increases in material wealth and prosperity. Between 1980 and 2005 the world economy grew at a steady pace despite several major disruptions including the Latin American debt crisis, the demise of the Soviet Union, the East Asia crisis, two global downturns, and the tragedy of September 11, 2001. Fortunately strong income growth was not only limited to developed countries. Income growth was especially strong in South and East Asia, but other developing regions were also able to realize strong increases in output. As a consequence the percentage of people living on less than $1 a day fell according to World Bank estimates from almost 27.9% of the population of developing countries to 18.4% (World Bank 2007).

Although these percentage reductions in poverty rates are important improvements, it is the absolute number of poor persons that is recognized in the public. The still high total number of poor persons often leads to the impression that global inequality has increased in the past decades. It is therefore very important to note that despite strong population growth, the absolute number of poor persons has decreased from more than 1.2 billion people in 1990 to 984 million in 2004. For the first time the number of people that live on less than $1 a day is below a billion. But this can not distract from the fact that still some 2.6 billion people, or almost half the developing world's population, remain below the $2 a day poverty line (World Bank 2007).

It is also extremely important to keep in mind that poverty is not limited to the income dimension but encompasses aspects such as a low life expectancy, high child mortality and undernutrition rates. Differences in these dimensions between developing and developed regions are enormous as well. While in rich countries fewer than 1 child in 100 does not reach its fifth birthday, in the poorest countries as many as a fifth of children do not. And while in rich countries fewer than 5 percent of all children under five are malnourished, in poor countries as many as 50 percent are.

The Fight against Poverty

In times of increasing opulence in the developed countries as well as in certain population subgroups in developing countries, the persistence of significant percentages of world population in poverty becomes more and more unacceptable. Consequentially this has lead to a lot of political activism. Numerous national and international organizations have formulated goals on how much poverty has to be reduced within the next decades, politicians have demanded time and again that development aid has to be increased dramatically, "Live-8"-Concerts have received a lot of public attention and celebrities as Bono are considered as "poverty experts".

Although globalization promises to improve the lot of humanity as a whole incalculably, there are signs of a backlash abound. The strong opposition against globalization is on the one hand due to the fact that in the rich world labor's share of GDP has fallen to historic lows, while profits are soaring, and on the other hand due to the persistence of absolute poverty in developing countries. Reductions in poverty rates are consequently not only a very worthy goal on their own, but an equitable distribution of globalization's profits is also the precondition for the general acceptance of liberal market economies.

Unfortunately not only the views of many adversaries of globalization but also most demands publicly announced by well-meaning politicians and celebrities are neither very realistic nor very likely to have the assumed positive effects on the poor. Although poverty in its many dimensions is clearly a very emotional topic, the fight against poverty should not be dominated by those expressing the most ambitious goals but by realism and scientific insights into the determinants of poverty.

Besides it is important to keep in mind that despite large income increases in the past and likely further increases in the future, that have the potential to lift a lot of of people out of poverty, it cannot be neglected that resources are scarce and will remain so in the future. This is especially the case when we take into account that poverty is not the only problem that has to be tackled in the coming decades. Considerable resources have to be devoted for example to the fight against communicable and non-communicable diseases like HIV/AIDS and Malaria or the fight against global warming.

Prioritization and Efficiency

Due to the scarcity of resources a certain degree of prioritization is necessary. Although prioritization is certainly necessary, the resentment against this idea is widespread. Mainly this is due to the general notion that we shouldn't have to prioritize. Whereas all demands for improvement in certain or all areas are uncontroversial, efforts for prioritization not only say where we should do more, but also where we shouldn't increase our efforts for the time being. This is then often seen as cynical. [1]

To be able to prioritize appropriately it is necessary to implement a cost-benefit analysis to be able to find the most efficient usage of the limited resources. The main precondition for this is a good knowledge about the determinants and the best policies to fight each problem. But before being able to analyze the determinants of the different global problems and especially of poverty it is of fundamental importance to find the right indicators for each phenomenon. Due to the multidimensionality of poverty there is a very large number of potential indicators and measurement issues are far from solved.

This thesis will try to contribute to the discussion of appropriate poverty indicators. All four essays are concerned with measurement issues of the different dimensions of poverty or are contributing to the literature on the determinants of poverty. While the first essay is focused on the appropriate measurement of changes in income poverty, namely changes in the Foster-Greer-Thorbecke (FGT) indicators of poverty, and the determinants of the size of these changes, the second essay is concerned with finding a meaningful indicator for undernutrition. Generally a large set of potential indicators for the measurement of undernutrition exists, but almost all suffer from certain biases and limitations. The second essay will try to shed some light on these problems and will give a clear recommendation on what indicator should be used to measure undernutrition and its changes over time. Besides income poverty and undernutrition, child mortality is a very important third dimension of poverty. Although the measurement of infant or child mortality is less controversial, knowledge on the determinants of this phenomenon can still be improved. The same is true for the determinants of undernutrition. Besides it is unclear how closely these two different dimensions of poverty - undernutrition and child mortality - are related.

To be able to track progress in different poverty dimensions and to give a better picture of the general development status of a country different multidimensional indicators were developed. Probably the most prominent example of such an indicator is the Human Development Index. But even this often cited indicator is far from universally accepted and it is criticized in different ways. One of the most controversial aspects of the HDI is the use of average values for each country. The fourth and last essay tries to allow for such criticism and develops a methodology to create an distribution sensitive Human Development Index.

---

[1]There have been very laudable efforts by the Copenhagen Consensus Project to establish a framework in which solutions to problems are prioritized based upon economic and scientific analysis of distinct subjects. The final 10 challenges found to hold the most promising opportunities include different dimensions of poverty, like communicable diseases, access to education, malnutrition and hunger and sanitation and access to clean water.

The Measurement of Changes in Income Poverty

Clearly one of the most important measurement issues of poverty is related to the measurement of poverty on the aggregate or macro level. The measures most often used to calculate the prevalence of poverty are the FGT poverty indicators. To be able to asses the impact of growth and distributional change on poverty reduction in a comparable manner for all countries, the relationship between growth, distributional change, and poverty reduction must be studied in a way that allows for country heterogeneity but remains tractable.

Although the usual measure of choice to analyze changes of poverty over time is the poverty elasticity, we propose an alternative measure to calculate the effects of income growth and distributional changes on poverty. Instead of studying the determinants of the percentage change in poverty (and the associated poverty elasticity of growth and distributional change), it is proposed to study the percentage point change in poverty (and the associated poverty semi-elasticity of growth and distributional change). It is argued that there are two distinct advantages to study absolute rather than proportionate poverty reductions. The first set of arguments is conceptual and relate to the fact that a strong bias is inherent in growth and distribution elasticities and that policy-makers are likely to be more interested in the percentage point changes in poverty rather than percent changes. The second set of arguments is empirical. It is shown that the estimation of semi-elasticities of growth and distributional changes on poverty rates is more precise. Besides using semi-elasticities avoids some arbitrary assumptions about excluding data from countries with low poverty incidence.

The Measurement of Undernutrition

A second dimension of poverty is the insufficient intake of energy through food and consequently the incidence of undernutrition. As undernutrition is a very severe and unacceptable dimension of poverty, the world community committed itself in the Millennium Development Goals (MDG) to reduce the number of people who suffer from hunger by half until 2015. The decision was made to use two different indicators to track progress with respect to the incidence of undernutrition. The first indicator is the FAO measure of access to an insufficient amount of calories. Unfortunately, there are considerable methodological as well as conceptual doubts about this FAO measure. The second measure used in the MDGs is 'underweight', which is an anthropometric indicator that measures the weight of a child for a certain age and compares it to a reference standard to be able to categorize a child as undernourished or not.

As Essay 2 argues, the choice of underweight as main indicator for the hunger dimension of poverty is not very fortunate. On the one hand, there are doubts about the general construction and interpretation of underweight that make it not very suitable to be used as a summary indicator. On the other hand, and this will be the main focus of this section, we can observe a bias in the development of underweight prevalence rates that is due to the large changes in the nutritional composition of diets in developing countries that are taking place. This so called 'nutrition transition' is characterized in large increases in the consumption of processed and semi-processed foods, that contain higher percentages of cheap fatty acids. Although this certainly means that total energy amounts taken up by children are increasing this should not be equalized with real improvements in their nutritional situation. This bias could lead to wrong conclusions concerning the fulfillment of the undernutrition aspect of MDG I.

Besides in 2006 a new multi-country reference standard was published by WHO. It is very likely that future progress in the fight against undernutrition will be tracked by using this new standard. The use of the new reference standard will result in clear changes in the prevalence and composition of undernutrition. Essay 2 therefore argues that this opportunity should be used to switch to stunting or a Composite Index of Anthropometric Failure instead of underweight as the main indicator to measure progress in the fight against hunger.

The Relationship between Undernutrition and Child Mortality

Poverty and changes in poverty are determined by various household, individual socio-economic and demographic characteristics as well as by various environmental factors. Essay 3, which is based on joint work with Kenneth Harttgen, is concerned both with the regional differences and the interdependencies of the outcomes and determinants of two of the most important poverty dimensions, namely child mortality and child undernutrition in South Asia and Sub-Saharan Africa. Child mortality and undernutrition remain still on a high level both in South Asia and Sub-Saharan Africa. Arguing that child mortality and undernutrition are highly correlated, i.e that a bad nutritional status of the child strongly increases the child's mortality risk (see e.g. Pelletier et al, 1995), a puzzle arises when comparing the two regions regarding the outcomes of both phenomena. Anthropometric outcomes of children are considerably better (but still on a very low level) in Sub-Saharan Africa than in South Asia. In contrast to the severe anthropometric failure in South Asia, Sub-Saharan African countries suffer from relatively high rates of child mortality (see e.g. Klasen, 2007; Ramalingaswami et al, 1996). This regional puzzle of child mortality and undernutrition between both regions is called the South Asia - Sub-Saharan Africa Enigma. To shed more light on this puzzle and the underlying reasons is of particular relevance. First, it would allow a much more detailed assessment of what is needed to reduce child mortality and undernutrition in these two regions. Second, it could show how strong child mortality and undernutrition are correlated and whether it is really sufficient to reduce undernutrition in order to reach the goal of reducing child mortality. Approaches using macro-data have not been able to explain the South Asia - Sub-Saharan Africa Enigma appropriately, however, and less attention has been paid so far to the analysis of determinants of undernutrition and child mortality based on micro-data, i.e population based household survey data.

Essay 3 analyzes the determinants of child mortality as well as of child undernutrition based on large-scale Demographic and Health Surveys (DHS) data for a sample of five developing countries in South Asia and Sub-Saharan Africa, namely Bangladesh, India, Uganda, Mali, and Zimbabwe. In particular, Essay 3 investigates the effects of a set of individual, household and cluster socioeconomic characteristics both on child mortality and undernutrition based on the analytical framework proposed by Mosley and Chen (1984). The aim of the paper is helping to explain the South Asia - Sub-Saharan Africa Enigma. To achieve this, first, Essay 3 analyzes the relationships between child mortality and undernutrition. The aim of this analysis is, first, to identify determinants that affect child mortality and undernutrition in different ways, which would help to explain the South Asia Sub-Sahara Africa Enigma. Second, analyzing the determinants of child mortality and undernutrition, Essay 3 concentrates on region-specific and country-specific differences both in the outcomes and determinants of both phenomena. This allows one to identify major differences that drives the puzzle of child mortality and undernutrition in the two regions and between countries. The main result of Essay 3 is the identification of several determinants that differ significantly from each other regarding their impact on child mortality and undernutrition, regarding the two regions of South Asia and Sub-Saharan Africa, and also regarding countries within the two regions. Whereas the access to health infrastructure is relatively more important ro reduce the risk of child mortality than the reduce the risk of undernutrition, the nutritional status of the mother, which is worse in South Asia than in Sub-Saharan Africa, has a much higher impact on child undernutrition than on child mortality, which can partly explain the Enigma.

The Multidimensional Measurement of Poverty

As the preceding sections have shown, poverty has many faces and can be measured in different ways and by using different indicators. The most well known indicator that takes this multidimensionality of poverty into consideration is the Human Development Index published by the United Nations Development Program (UNDP). One of the most often heard critiques of the HDI is that is does not take into account inequality within countries in its three dimensions. In Essay 4 a relatively easy and intuitive approach which allows to compute the three components and the overall HDI for quintiles of the income distribution is therefore suggested. This allows to compare the level in human development of the poor with the level of the non-poor within countries, but also across countries. An empirical illustration for a sample of 14 low and middle income countries as well as Finland and the United States shows that inequality in human development within countries is indeed high.

When examining the individual components it becomes clear that the biggest effect of inequality on the quintile-specific HDI is in the income component. In many countries the richest quintile has an income that is often more than twice or even up to five times as high as among the poorest quintile. Here many of the Sub-Saharan African countries have the highest inequality, followed closely by the Latin American. The differential in educational achievements between the richest and the poorest quintile are also sizeable, but smaller than in the income index. The smallest differential is found in life expectancy achievements, although the differential is still very substantial.

Although among rich countries all three differentials are considerably smaller, the results also show that the level of inequality is not directly linked to the level of human development itself. Comparing the rank positions of the different quintiles this point. For example the richest quintile in Bolivia is at rank 34, i.e. among the countries with the high human development, whereas the poorest quintile is at rank 132. The average HDI of Bolivia was in last year's report at rank 112. Looking at a developed country like the US shows, that the richest quintile would top the list of human development achievements, whereas the poorest quintile in the USA only achieves rank 48, considerably worse off than the richest quintile in South Africa, Bolivia or Indonesia.

Essay 1

The Semi-Elasticity of Poverty Reduction

Abstract: In this paper we examine the mathematical relationship between growth and distributional change on absolute (i.e. percentage point) changes in FGT poverty measures assuming a log-normal distribution. We also test the empirical relationship of the derived semi-elasticities of growth and distributional change on poverty and find them to explain changes in poverty very well (in fact, better than a related study by Bourguignon (2003) that studied the 'regular' growth elasticity of poverty reduction). This relationship will allow us to predict where growth and distributional change will have the largest (absolute) impact on poverty reduction, which is very useful for predicting and analyzing progress towards meeting MDG1.

---

based on joint work with Stephan Klasen.

1.1 Introduction

Prospects for poverty reduction in regions and on the global level, which are critical for assessing progress towards meeting the first Millennium Development Goal, have so fare relied largely on simple extrapolations (e.g. Ravallion and Chen, 2004). At the same time, we know quite a bit more about the impact of growth and distributional change on poverty reduction and these insights could be used to assess prospects for poverty reduction, depending on particular country circumstances and growth scenarios. To provide such assessments in a comparable manner for all countries, the relationship between growth, distributional change, and poverty reduction must be studied in a way that allows for country heterogeneity but remains tractable.

Discussions about the sensitivity of the incidence of poverty to economic growth have been going on for a number of years (e.g. World Bank, 2000; Ravallion and Datt 1998, Bourguignon, 2003). Although most studies clearly show that growth reduces poverty, the size of this effect is still debated (e.g. Dollar and Kraay, 2002). Whereas different studies estimated the growth elasticity of poverty reduction to be somewhere between -2.0 and -3.0 (Ravallion and Chen, 1997; Bruno, Ravallion and Squire, 1998; World Bank 2000) a well known study by Bhalla (2002) estimated it to be about -5.0, meaning that a 1 percent increase in mean income reduces the poverty headcount by 5 percent.

A related question concerns the impact of distributional change on poverty. While also here there has been some empirical work (e.g. reviewed in World Bank 2000 and Bourguignon, 2003), the purely data-driven approaches have usually yielded mixed and strongly varying estimates and are often only able to explain a small portion of the actual change in poverty. In particular, it has become increasingly clear that both the impact of growth and distributional change on poverty will depend on a number of factors, including the location of the poverty line and the initial level of inequality.

From an analytical point of view this is not very surprising, since an identity links changes in mean income, changes in the income distribution and reductions in poverty. This identity results in a non-linear relationship between economic growth and headcount poverty as well as between distributional changes and headcount poverty [1]. Although the identity has been known for quite a while, only a small number of studies has taken account of it, namely Ravallion and Huppi (1991), Datt and Ravallion (1992), Kakwani (1993) and Bourguignon (2003). All these studies are limited to the country level with the only exception being Bourguignon (2003). This is due to the fact that one needs to know the complete

---

[1] In the following it will be shown that the identity can be used to calculate the influence of income and distribution changes on other poverty measures than the headcount poverty ratio as for example the FGT poverty measures.

distribution of incomes on the household level. Bourguignon (2003) circumvents this problem by assuming that incomes are lognormally distributed and therefore the complete distribution of incomes is known as long as information on mean income and the Gini coefficient is available. With this simplifying assumption, one can mathematically determine the poverty elasticity to growth and distributional change and it will depend on initial inequality, as well as the location of the poverty line in relation to mean incomes. It turns out that this simplification fits the data extremely well (see Bourguignon, 2003) and this is also supported by our calculations using a similar (and partially overlapping) dataset used by Adams (2004) which is also based on the World Bank poverty monitoring database. Thus the assumption of log-normality achieves the goal of providing a simple, yet powerful tool to assess and project poverty reduction depending on country circumstances.

Using the same assumption as Bourguignon (2003) we propose an alternative measure to calculate the effects of income growth and distributional changes on poverty. Instead of studying the determinants of the percentage change in poverty (and the associated poverty elasticity of growth and distributional change), we propose to study the percentage point change in poverty (and the associated poverty semi-elasticity of growth and distributional change). We argue that there are two distinct advantages to study absolute rather than proportionate poverty reduction. The first set of arguments is conceptual. They relate to the fact that policy-makers are likely to be more interested in the percentage point changes in poverty rather than percent changes [2]. Also, when the poverty incidence becomes small, large percentage changes in poverty incidence are easily achieved and it seems difficult to treat poverty reduction from an incidence of 2 to 1 percent in the same manner as poverty reduction from an incidence of 80 to 40%. Lastly, as discussed further below, it can be shown that in growing countries (and a constant real absolute poverty line), the growth elasticity of poverty reduction will keep going up, giving the misleading impression of growth not only being 'good for the poor', but becoming ever better for them over time.

The second set of arguments is empirical. We show below that one can estimate the semi-elasticities of growth and distributional change on poverty reduction much more precisely and does not need to make arbitrary assumptions about excluding data from countries with low poverty incidence. Also, such analysis will place more weight on countries with high poverty incidence which is desirable as these countries are the main concern of the international poverty reduction effort. Moreover, percentage changes in poverty are influenced much more by

---

[2]One may argue that MDG1 is, at the global level, about percentage changes in poverty (i.e. a 50% reduction in poverty). But since progress will be uneven between countries, it will be much easier to understand progress if one reformulated the goal as an absolute reduction in the poverty incidence from 29% to 14.5% and then consider what absolute poverty reduction where would contribute by how much to this goal.

observations with low poverty incidence which are highly susceptible to measurement error in the left tail of the income distribution and could therefore bias the results.

In section 1.2 we briefly review the mathematical relationships between growth, distributional change, and poverty reduction under the log-normal assumption, using both the proportionate as well as the absolute change in poverty. In section 1.3 we consider the relative merits of the elasticity versus the semi-elasticity in more detail. In section 1.4, we move to the data and study to what extent we are able to explain past absolute and relative poverty reduction with the log-normal assumption. In the last section we conclude and assess prospects for poverty reduction in different countries of the world, based on the existing income and distribution patterns.

1.2   Influence of Income and Distribution Changes

Figure 1.1: Decomposition

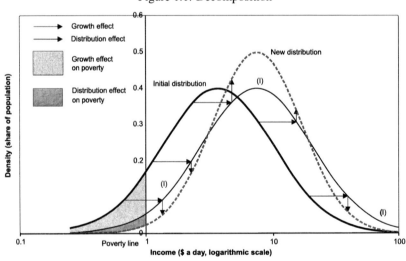

Source: Bourguignon (2003).

As already mentioned by Bourguignon (2003), Datt and Ravallion (1992) and others, poverty reductions are either due to increases in mean income or changes in the distribution of relative incomes. Knowing this, any change in headcount poverty can be decomposed into a) a "growth effect" that is the result of a proportional change in all incomes that leaves the distribution of relative incomes unaffected and b) a "distributional effect" that is only due to a change in the distribution of relative incomes leaving the mean income constant. These two effects are shown in Fig. 1.1. It is discernable that the estimation of the two effects will exhibit path dependence.

Formally the change in headcount poverty can be explained by the following decomposition identity:

$$\Delta H = H_{t'} - H_t = \left[\tilde{F}_t \left(\frac{z}{\bar{y}_{t'}} \right) - \tilde{F}_t \left(\frac{z}{\bar{y}_t} \right) \right] + \left[\tilde{F}_{t'} \left(\frac{z}{\bar{y}_{t'}} \right) - \tilde{F}_t \left(\frac{z}{\bar{y}_{t'}} \right) \right] \quad (1.1)$$

Using the empirically plausible assumption proposed by Bourguignon (2003) that incomes are lognormally distributed, we no longer need to know the total distribution of individual incomes to calculate headcount poverty. The only information necessary is the mean income yt, the constant international poverty line z (e.g. the $1 a day criterion) and the standard deviation of the lognormal distribution :

$$H_t = \tilde{F}_t(log(z/\bar{y}_t)) = \Pi \left[\frac{log(z/\bar{y}_t)}{\sigma} + \frac{1}{2}\sigma \right]. \quad (1.2)$$

wherein Π is the cumulative distribution function of the standard normal. The standard deviation of the lognormal distribution can be calculated from the Gini coefficient by the following equation:

$$\sigma = \sqrt{2} \left[\Pi^{-1} \left(\frac{G+1}{2} \right) \right] \quad (1.3)$$

Besides the headcount poverty ratio at a certain point in time, relative and absolute changes in poverty due to "growth effects" and "distributional effects" can be formally studied by considering the poverty impact of changes in mean income and changes in the income distribution. When considering relative changes in the headcount poverty ratio, the growth elasticity of poverty reduction is given by

$$\varepsilon_y^H = \frac{\Delta H}{\Delta log(\bar{y})H_t} = \frac{1}{\sigma}\lambda \left[\frac{log(z/\bar{y}_t)}{\sigma} + \frac{1}{2}\sigma \right] \quad (1.4)$$

where λ is the hazard rate, which is the ratio of density function to the cumulative density function of the standard normal.

Similarly the distribution elasticity of poverty reduction is given by

$$\varepsilon_\sigma^H = \lambda \left[\frac{log(z/\bar{y}_t)}{\sigma} + \frac{1}{2}\sigma \right] \cdot \left[\frac{1}{2} - \frac{log(z/\bar{y}_t)}{\sigma^2} \right]. \quad (1.5)$$

In contrast to Bourguignon, our focus will be on absolute (i.e. percentage point) changes in the headcount poverty ratio and therefore on semi-elasticities. As will be argued below this is a less misleading measure than elasticities. Using equation (1) the growth semi-elasticity of poverty reduction is

$$\kappa_y = \frac{1}{\sigma}\pi\left[\frac{log(z/\bar{y}_t)}{\sigma} + \frac{1}{2}\sigma\right]\tag{1.6}$$

and the semi-elasticity due to distributional changes in relative incomes is given by

$$\kappa_\sigma = \pi\left[\frac{log(z/\bar{y}_t)}{\sigma} + \frac{1}{2}\sigma\right]\cdot\left[\frac{1}{2} - \frac{log(z/\bar{y}_t)}{\sigma^2}\right],\tag{1.7}$$

where π is the density function of the standard normal.

When combined with the growth rate and the percentage change in the standard deviation, respectively these theoretical values of the semi-elasticities will identify the percentage point changes in the headcount poverty ratio either due to growth in mean income (5) or due to changes in the distribution of relative incomes (6) depending on the level of development and the existing distribution of incomes.

As mentioned before, it is also possible to calculate the elasticities and semi-elasticities for the other FGT-measures. According to formulas derived by Kakwani (1993) the elasticity η_{P_α} of FGT-measure P_α with respect to changes in mean income is

$$\eta_{P_\alpha} = \frac{\delta P_\alpha}{\delta\mu}\frac{\mu}{P_\alpha} = -\frac{\alpha[P_{\alpha-1} - P_\alpha]}{P_\alpha}\tag{1.8}$$

The elasticity ε_{P_α} of a FGT-measure with respect to a change in the distribution leaving the mean income unaffected can be denoted by the following equation

$$\varepsilon_{P_\alpha} = \eta_{P_\alpha} + \frac{\alpha\mu P_{\alpha-1}}{z P_\alpha}\tag{1.9}$$

In combination with the assumption of lognormally distributed incomes this means that the elasticity of the poverty gap with respect to changes in mean come is the following and depends partly on the mean income of the poor $\bar{y}_t^*$ [3]:

$$\varepsilon_y^{PG} = -\frac{\Pi[\frac{log(z/\bar{y}_t)}{\sigma} + \frac{1}{2}\sigma]}{(\frac{z}{\bar{y}_t^*})\cdot\Pi[\frac{log(z/\bar{y}_t)}{\sigma} + \frac{1}{2}\sigma] - \Pi[\frac{log(z/\bar{y}_t)}{\sigma} + \frac{1}{2}\sigma]}\tag{1.10}$$

---

[3]It should be noted that identity 1.10 differs from the formula cited by Bourguignon (2003), in which the mean income of the poor is not explicitly taken into consideration.

Using the formulas derived by Kakwani (1993) we can also generate values for the semi-elasticities of the FGT-measures, which are with respect to income

$$\kappa_y^{P_\alpha} = \varepsilon_y^{P_\alpha} * P_\alpha = -\alpha[P_{\alpha-1} - P_\alpha] \tag{1.11}$$

and with respect to changes in distribution

$$\kappa_\sigma^{P_\alpha} = \alpha P_\alpha + \alpha(\frac{\mu}{z} - 1)P_{\alpha-1}. \tag{1.12}$$

1.3 Growth Elasticity versus Semi-Elasticity

Economists usually tend to use elasticities to measure the influence of income/consumption growth on poverty changes. Although this information is clearly of some relevance it is actually absolute changes in poverty measures and therefore semi-elasticities that policy makers at the national and international level are interested in. The amount of persons leaving or entering poverty measured as a percentage of the total population is clearly of more interest than the same amount measured as a percentage of the poor. Stated differently the reduction of the percentage of the population that is living below the poverty line by 10 percentage points is clearly a lot. But the reduction of headcount poverty by 10% can be a lot, if the poverty rate is currently around 60%, but if it is only at 6% it is not really that much (only another 0.6% of the population are leaving poverty). [4]

Moreover, as shown in the formulas above, the growth elasticity of poverty reduction is highly sensitive to the location of the poverty line relative to mean incomes. For example the continuous progress in the economic development of developing countries will lead to an increase in the distance between poverty line and mean incomes, equivalent to a reduction in headcount poverty. This reduction of the level of poor will lead to general increases in the elasticity due to the lower base by which absolute poverty changes are divided. This may lead policy makers to the conclusion that policies that were implemented in times with lower poverty rates were more successful in poverty reduction than policies that were implemented during times of very high poverty rates, although these changes are purely a consequence of the way elasticities are calculated. To give an easy imaginary example, future economists might find that growth elasticities between 1980 and 2000 were a lot lower than in the following two decades. Therefore they might falsely come to the conclusion that the growth enhancing policies implemented in the last two decades were less successful than growth policies that are to be implemented in the future. In contrast, the semi-elasticity formulation will not

---

[4]One could also focus on the absolute number of poor persons, which is clearly of considerable policy relevance.

have an in-built increase in the poverty impact of growth. In fact, the opposite occurs. As countries grow richer, the ability of growth to achieve the same absolute poverty reduction becomes increasingly smaller which seems more plausible as it becomes increasingly difficult to improve the plight of few remaining desperately poor in a society.

From an empirical point of view, there are further advantages to estimating the determinants of absolute rather than proportionate changes in poverty. In estimating the determinants of proportionate changes in welfare, Bourguignon states that he had to 'eliminate all spells where the percentage change in poverty headcount was abnormally large in relative value' (Bourguignon 2003). Also, all observations where poverty was 0 in the first period can also not be considered. Using the semi-elasticity, we can include all observations that are available and are not bound by such an arbitrary decision. In our case we can increase the number of growth and poverty spells from 102 to 125. In particular, we are able to include many growth spells from Eastern Europe and Central Asia which would otherwise be under-represented in the dataset.

Another positive consequence of using semi-elasticities is a better fit when considering other poverty measures such as the poverty gap and squared poverty gap. This is an issue that will become apparent in the empirical findings below.

1.4   Empirical Results

In the empirical section we test our ability to explain the determinants of absolute and relative poverty change using the above formulas. We do this using a slightly different data-set which is an updated version of the World Bank Poverty Monitoring data set also used by Adams (2004). To make our results easily comparable with those of Bourguignon we have used the same set of regressions and given them the same names. In Tab. 1.1 - 1.6 our first regression is the naïve model that tries to explain changes in poverty measures by changes in mean incomes only. In all cases growth clearly has a significant poverty reducing effect but only a small part of the variation in poverty changes can be explained by a linear influence of mean income growth. The second regression in Tab. 1.1 - 1.6 is the so called standard model that also takes changes in the distribution of incomes (i.e. variations in the Gini coefficient) into consideration and improves the fit of all models.

As shown in the formulas above, both changes in mean incomes as well as changes in distribution have a non-constant influence on changes in poverty measures. As the formulas show, the size of the effects depends on the position of the poverty line relative to mean income and on initial inequality. This non-linear influence of growth in mean incomes is considered by interacting growth with the initial poverty-line/mean-income ratio and the initial Gini coefficient (Improved

Table 1.1: Absolute change in headcount poverty rate during growth spell

	Naive Model	Standard Model	Improved Standard Model 1	Improved Standard Model 2	Identity Model 1	Identity Model 2
Intercept	-0.0035	-0.0123	0.0001	0.0069	0.0007	0.0096
	-0.50	-1.92	0.01	1.41	0.15	2.08
Y = % change in mean income	-0.1769	-0.1462	0.2837	0.1612		
	-6.53	-5.94	4.06	2.54		
DGini = Variation in Gini		0.1947	0.2569	0.0168	0.2443	
		5.87	9.31	0.38	9.83	
Y * pov.line/mean-inc.			-0.8954	-0.8617		
			-6.95	-7.73		
Y * initial Gini			-0.5602	-0.3036		
			-2.88	-1.75		
DGini * poverty-line/mean-income				0.0088		
				2.26		
DGini * initial Gini				0.0123		
				3.01		
Y * theoretical value of gse* (lognormal assumption)					-0.9901	-1.0419
					-12.09	-13.29
DSigma * theor. value of pise** (lognormal assumption)						0.7330
						10.87
R^2	0.2571	0.4207	0.6368	0.7331	0.6601	0.6906
Adj. R^2	0.2511	0.4112	0.6247	0.7196	0.6546	0.6856
Obs.	125	125	125	125	125	125

Notes: *gse = growth semi-elasticity. **pise = poverty inequality semi-elasticity.

Standard Model 1). By interacting changes in the Gini coefficient with the same two factors we also take account of the non-linear influence of changes in the distribution of incomes (Improved Standard Model 2). When taking these non-linear influences of growth and distribution changes into consideration we are able to explain more than 70% of the variation in absolute changes in headcount poverty (Table 1.1) and about 50% of the variation in relative changes in headcount poverty (Table 1.2). This is a considerably improvement. The greater explanatory power of the regressions of the absolute poverty change is also true if we restricted the data set to the 102 observations used in the relative regression.

While in these first four regressions no assumptions are made on how income growth interacts with the distance of the poverty line to mean income and the initial degree of inequality the fifth regression (Identity Model 1) assumes a joint effect of these three variables according to the theoretical (semi-)elasticity men-

Table 1.2: Relative change in headcount poverty rate during growth spell

	Naive Model	Standard Model	Improved Standard Model 1	Improved Standard Model 2	Identity Model 1	Identity Model 2
Intercept	0.5266	0.4782	0.3429	0.2278	0.3877	0.1903
	2.46	2.37	1.76	1.23	2.18	1.58
Y = % change in mean income	-4.1283	-4.5748	-21.3351	-22.3100		
	-4.28	-4.99	-4.37	-5.20		
DGini = Variation in Gini		5.3861	5.7352	36.5913	5.6641	
		3.71	4.13	5.96	4.42	
Y * poverty-line/mean-income			16.2323	17.2438		
			2.98	3.61		
Y * initial Gini			28.3531	29.1387		
			2.82	3.30		
DGini * poverty-line/mean-income				-30.5798		
				-4.63		
DGini * initial Gini				-44.7220		
				-3.55		
Y * theoretical value of gse* (lognormal assumption)					-2.0519	-1.6908
					-7.72	-9.48
DSigma * theor. value of pise** (lognormal assumption)						1.1989
						12.76
R^2	0.1546	0.2580	0.3491	0.5110	0.4201	0.7374
Adj. R^2	0.1462	0.2430	0.3223	0.4801	0.4084	0.7321
Obs.	102	102	102	102	102	102

Notes: *gse = growth semi-elasticity. **pise = poverty inequality semi-elasticity.

tioned in section 1.3. The last regression model (Identity Model 2) further assumes a joint effect of a change in the distribution, the development level and the initial degree of inequality according to the theoretical (semi-)elasticity. As seen in Table 1.1 and Table 1.2 the assumption of a lognormal distribution fits the data very well. Multiplying growth in mean incomes with the respective theoretical value for the (semi-)elasticity and multiplying a change in the distribution of incomes with its respective theoretical value for the (semi-)elasticity can explain in both cases about 70% of the variation in absolute/relative changes in headcount poverty rates.

Whereas the results for headcount poverty are very similar between the last regressions in Tables 1.1 and 1.2, the goodness of fit is a lot better when looking at absolute changes in poverty gap and squared poverty gap and therefore when semi-elasticities are considered (Tables 3 and 5). The R^2 values in Tables 1.3 to 1.6, where relative changes in poverty gap and squared poverty gap are considered, respectively, are quite modest, suggesting that the lognormal assumption is no longer as suitable because the explanatory power of the Identity Models are in both cases considerably smaller than those of the Improved Standard Models. The likely reason for the poor fit when considering depth and distribution-sensitive poverty measures is that the increasing importance of the left tail of the distribution in these poverty measures where observations from countries with low poverty incidence are particularly influential and particularly prone to measurement error in the left tail of the distribution. An alternative way of phrasing the issue is that the assumption of log-normality is probably particularly error-prone the more one moves into the left tail of the distribution. In the relative poverty change regressions, the left tail from low incidence countries are particularly influential and this might therefore explain the poor fit. In contrast, it is very encouraging to see that we are able to explain changes in the absolute poverty gap and poverty severity very well still with the log-normal assumption. Thus our simplifying assumption of log-normality works particularly well when trying to explain absolute changes in poverty.

The preceding empirical results are very encouraging and allow us to generate tables for policy makers that could give a clear impression as to what percent point reduction in headcount poverty a 1% growth in mean incomes yields depending on the initial Gini coefficient and the level of development (Table 1.7).

Similar tables can also be generated for changes in the distribution of incomes as well as for other FGT-measures. These tables are shown in Tables A1 to A4 in Appendix A.

Table 1.7 shows that the impact of growth on absolute (percentage point) poverty reduction is particularly large for countries where the poverty line is close to mean incomes and the level of inequality is low. Table 1.8 shows the elasticities and semi-elasticities for a number of individual countries to illustrate the difference with concrete country examples. When we study elasticities, by far the largest effects are found in the transition countries where poverty incidence is very low. In contrast, the highest semi-elasticities are found in Bangladesh, Ethiopia, Pakistan, and India. Thus we could expect that growth and pro-poor distributional change will lead to the largest effects on absolute poverty reduction in these countries and thus to the largest impact on poverty reduction at the global level. This not only generates a totally different picture on the impact of growth on poverty than suggested by the elasticities but it also puts into perspective recent debates about India's success in reducing poverty (e.g. Bhalla 2002; Bhalla 2003; Deaton 2003a, Deaton 2003b). It appears that India was benefiting from being precisely in the situation where its growth will have the largest absolute impact on poverty.

Table 1.3: Absolute change in poverty gap ratio during growth spell

	Naive Model	Standard Model	Improved Standard Model 1	Improved Standard Model 2	Identity Model 1	Identity Model 2
Intercept	-0.1893	-0.6600	0.1307	0.4616	0.0261	0.8068
	-0.46	-1.72	0.43	1.85	0.08	3.30
Y = % change in mean income	-8.0477	-6.4003	19.9626	10.6787		
	-5.06	-4.33	4.96	3.31		
DGini = Variation in Gini		10.4652	14.3797	-1.8911	12.1874	
		5.25	9.06	-0.84	7.95	
Y * poverty-line/mean-income			-59.2421	-56.7783		
			-8.00	-10.02		
Y * initial Gini			-31.0163	-11.8068		
			-2.77	-1.34		
DGini * poverty-line/mean-income				1.0293		
				5.21		
DGini * initial Gini				0.4677		
				2.24		
Y * theoretical value of gse* (lognormal assumption)					-1.1187	-1.1476
					-10.25	-12.82
DSigma * theor. value of pise** (lognormal assumption)						1.7043
						12.39
R^2	0.1721	0.3247	0.6117	0.7771	0.5813	0.7185
Adj. R^2	0.1653	0.3137	0.5987	0.7657	0.5745	0.7139
Obs.	125	125	125	125	125	125

Notes: *gse = growth semi-elasticity. **pise = poverty inequality semi-elasticity.

1.5   Conclusion

To summarize our results strong support is found for the assumption of lognormally distributed incomes. On the other hand the results show that the use of semi-elasticities instead of elasticities has considerable advantages aside from the fact that semi-elasticities are less prone to misinterpretations. By looking at absolute changes (i.e. percentage point changes) in headcount poverty, poverty gap and squared poverty gap we can increase the number of observations by about 20%. The generation of semi-elasticities needs no additional information and can be achieved by simple modifications of the formulas derived in Kakwani (1993). Besides the use of semi-elasticities leads to very high R^2 values even for distributionally sensitive measures like poverty gap and squared poverty gap. With our measure we come to drastically different interpretations of the prospects for

Table 1.4: Relative change in poverty gap ratio during growth spell

	Naive Model	Standard Model	Improved Standard Model 1	Improved Standard Model 2	Identity Model 1	Identity Model 2
Intercept	0.8454	0.8022	0.7712	0.7688	0.7089	0.7008
	2.72	2.63	2.46	2.24	2.26	2.22
Y = % change in mean income	-4.5943	-4.9930	-2.4044	-2.6994		
	-3.28	-3.60	-0.31	-0.34		
DGini = Variation in Gini		4.8088	4.5001	7.2457	4.5035	
		2.19	2.02	1.18	1.99	
Y * poverty-line/mean-income			5.2923	5.5254		
			0.60	0.63		
Y * initial Gini			-10.7182	-10.3106		
			-0.66	-0.63		
DGini * poverty-line/mean-income				-0.1799		
				-0.60		
DGini * initial Gini				0.1376		
				0.05		
Y * theoretical value of gse* (lognormal assumption)					-0.7561	-0.6978
					-2.52	-2.33
DSigma * theor. value of pise** (lognormal assumption)						1.7376
						1.73
R^2	0.0970	0.1388	0.1480	0.1516	0.0848	0.0761
Adj. R^2	0.0880	0.1214	0.1129	0.0980	0.0664	0.0574
Obs.	102	102	102	102	102	102

Notes: *gse = growth semi-elasticity. **pise = poverty inequality semi-elasticity.

poverty reduction in the future as well as on explaining the record of poverty reduction in different countries.

But at the same time it has to be kept in mind, that the results are not directly about policies. Therefore they give no hint as to what policies are of particular importance to the reduction of poverty rates. Besides the differentiation between growth and distribution effects is somehow artificial since almost no policy influences only growth or only the distribution of incomes. But despite these caveats the above elucidated method to assess the impacts on poverty rates across countries seems to be better suited than prior methods.

Table 1.5: Absolute change in squared poverty gap ratio during growth spell

	Naive Model	Standard Model	Improved Standard Model 1	Improved Standard Model 2	Identity Model 1	Identity Model 2
Intercept	-0.0634	-0.3592	0.1867	0.3657	0.0322	0.6071
	-0.21	*-1.25*	*0.79*	*1.84*	*0.13*	*2.89*
Y = % change in mean income	-4.8698	-3.8330	14.0963	7.616		
	-4.28	*-3.54*	*4.63*	*3.03*		
DGini = Variation in Gini		6.5542	9.2103	-1.5160	7.3959	
		4.48	*7.65*	*-0.86*	*6.11*	
Y * poverty-line/mean-income			-40.5948	-38.7195		
			-7.22	*-8.74*		
Y * initial Gini			-20.8864	-7.6895		
			-2.46	*-1.12*		
DGini * poverty-line/mean-income				0.8811		
				5.62		
DGini * initial Gini				0.1419		
				0.86		
Y * theoretical value of gse* (lognormal assumption)					-1.0922	-1.1214
					-7.96	*-9.29*
DSigma * theor. value of pise** (lognormal assumption)						1.4229
						9.08
R^2	0.1342	0.2611	0.5460	0.7232	0.4692	0.5892
Adj. R^2	0.1268	0.2485	0.5302	0.7085	0.4602	0.5821
Obs.	120	120	120	120	120	120

Notes: *gse = growth semi-elasticity. **pise = poverty inequality semi-elasticity.

Table 1.6: Relative change in squared poverty gap ratio during growth spell

	Naive Model	Standard Model	Improved Standard Model 1	Improved Standard Model 2	Identity Model 1	Identity Model 2
Intercept	1.4112	1.3266	1.3740	1.2107	1.2402	1.2062
	3.01	*2.96*	*2.99*	*2.43*	*2.70*	*2.60*
Y = % change in mean income	-4.3469	-5.2351	8.6458	7.6383		
	-2.08	*-2.60*	*0.77*	*0.68*		
DGini = Variation in Gini		10.1417	9.5971	20.5698	9.4710	
		3.20	*3.00*	*2.36*	*2.91*	
Y * poverty-line/mean-income			-4.6689	-4.1046		
			-0.37	*-0.32*		
Y * initial Gini			-30.8061	-29.5108		
			-1.32	*-1.26*		
DGini * poverty-line/mean-income				-0.3548		
				-0.84		
DGini * initial Gini				-.2884		
				-0.69		
Y * theoretical value of gse* (lognormal assumption)					-0.2312	-0.1714
					-1.07	*-0.80*
DSigma * theor. value of pise** (lognormal assumption)						1.9739
						2.74
R^2	0.0439	0.1390	0.1552	0.1725	0.0878	0.0793
Adj. R^2	0.0338	0.1205	0.1181	0.1168	0.0682	0.0595
Obs.	96	96	96	96	96	96

Notes: *gse = growth semi-elasticity. **pise = poverty inequality semi-elasticity.

Table 1.7: Poverty/Growth semi-elasticity as a function of mean income and income inequality

Gini	Poverty line as a proportion of mean income									
	0.10	0.20	0.30	0.40	0.50	0.60	0.70	0.80	0.90	1.00
0.20	0.000	0.000	0.007	0.066	0.239	0.512	0.798	1.009	1.106	1.096
0.25	0.000	0.003	0.044	0.173	0.374	0.586	0.754	0.854	0.885	0.863
0.30	0.000	0.020	0.112	0.271	0.444	0.587	0.681	0.725	0.730	0.705
0.35	0.003	0.057	0.185	0.337	0.466	0.555	0.605	0.621	0.614	0.590
0.40	0.013	0.107	0.245	0.370	0.459	0.511	0.535	0.537	0.524	0.502
0.45	0.033	0.158	0.286	0.379	0.436	0.464	0.472	0.466	0.451	0.432
0.50	0.064	0.201	0.307	0.372	0.405	0.418	0.416	0.406	0.391	0.373
0.55	0.100	0.233	0.313	0.354	0.371	0.032	0.366	0.354	0.340	0.324
0.60	0.137	0.252	0.307	0.330	0.335	0.331	0.321	0.308	0.295	0.281
0.65	0.168	0.258	0.293	0.302	0.299	0.291	0.280	0.267	0.255	0.243
0.70	0.192	0.255	0.271	0.271	0.263	0.253	0.241	0.230	0.219	0.208

Table 1.8: Country Comparisons of Elasticities and Semi-Elasticities

Country	Headcount poverty	Headcount poverty (theo.)	Gini Coeff.	Mean Income	Growth semi-elast.	Distr. semi-elast.	Growth elast.	Distr. elasticity
Brazil 1997	5.10	5.11	51.7	3250	0.106	0.278	2.070	5.435
India 1997	44.03	39.91	37.8	599	0.553	0.528	1.386	1.322
China (Urban) 1998	0.98	4.30	40.3	1875	0.122	0.301	2.841	7.001
China (Rural) 1998	24.14	34.08	40.3	706	0.491	0.568	1.439	1.666
Slovak Republic 1993	0.00	0.00	19.5	3014	0.000	0.000	16.694	100.343
Latvia 1995	0.00	0.11	28.5	2179	0.007	0.025	6.479	23.189
Lithuania 1993	16.47	19.01	33.6	814	0.441	0.659	2.321	3.464
Bangladesh 1992	35.86	35.94	28.3	539	0.730	0.637	2.032	1.771
Indonesia 1998	26.33	21.10	31.5	734	0.504	0.693	2.387	3.286
Niger 1995	61.42	64.83	50.6	434	0.384	0.225	0.592	0.347
Ethiopia 1995	31.25	33.39	40.0	710	0.491	0.575	1.471	1.721
Zambia 1993	69.16	72.12	46.2	344	0.386	0.110	0.535	0.152
Turkmenistan 1993	20.92	20.42	35.8	839	0.432	0.640	2.114	3.136
Pakistan 1993	33.90	34.03	34.2	619	0.585	0.607	1.720	1.785

Essay 2

Undernutrition and the Nutrition Transition

Abstract: Since the publication of the new multi-country reference standard by WHO it is likely that future progress in the fight against undernutrition will be tracked by using this new standard. The use of the new reference standard will result in clear changes in the prevalence and composition of undernutrition. This paper argues that this opportunity should be used to use stunting or a Composite Index of Anthropometric Failure instead of underweight as the indicator to measure progress in the fight against hunger. All weight based anthropometric measures, such as underweight and wasting, suffer from the fact that due to changes in the nutritional composition of diets in developing countries there is going to be a secular reduction in those measures that does not coincide with real improvements in the health of the affected children. This bias could lead to wrong conclusions concerning the fulfillment of the undernutrition aspect of MDG I.

2.1   Introduction

In September 2000, leaders from 189 countries adopted the eight Millennium Development Goals of which the most prominent goal is to eradicate extreme poverty
and hunger. To be able to track progress on this commitment a number of relevant
indicators was selected to be used to assess progress over the period from 1990
to 2015, when targets are expected to be met. With respect to hunger the explicit
goal is to halve the proportion of people who suffer from hunger. The decision
was made to use two different indicators to track progress with respect to the incidence of undernutrition. The first indicator is the FAO measure of access to an
insufficient amount of calories.

Due to the lack of appropriate information on the household level on caloric
availability, the FAO uses a macro approach that proceeds in three steps. In the
first step the per capita caloric availability in a country is calculated by estimating
food production (including auto-consumption), subtracting imports, making al-
lowances for waste and use as seed, and then transforming available food into its
caloric content. After dividing by population, per capita availability is computed
on a 3-year rolling average basis. In the second step, an estimation of the distribution of calories among households is performed, under the assumption of a log
normal distribution and with an estimate that takes into account inequality in food
expenditures. In the third step the average age-sex composition and activity levels are used to calculate the cut-off point which is then applied to the log-normal
distribution to calculate the share of undernourished persons [1] (Klasen 2007).

Unfortunately, there are considerable methodological as well as conceptual
doubts about this FAO measure. It especially remains unclear whether the FAO
measure of undernourishment really presents a reliable estimate of the proportion
of the population that is 'hungry' in a given year (see e.g. Klasen 2007; Svedberg
2002). Especially the geographical composition of undernutrition according to the
FAO measure stands in strong contrast to evidence from anthropometric measures
(Svedberg 1999, Klasen 2003). Therefore it is of considerable importance that the
second measure for undernutrition gives a better and more reliable picture about
the real incidence of undernutrition.

The second measure used in the MDGs is 'underweight', which is an anthropometric indicator that measures the weight of a child for a certain age and compares it to a reference standard to be able to categorize a child as undernourished
or not. The two other well known measures of effective nutritional status are stunting (height for age) and wasting (weight for height). Anthropometric indicators
have different advantages and drawbacks that are well known in the literature (see
especially Svedberg 2002, Klasen 2007). Probably the largest drawback of these

---

[1]For a detailed discussion of the method see Naiken (2003).

three anthropometric measures is, that information is almost entirely restricted to children up to the age of five years. Each of these three indicators measures a different aspect of undernutrition. While stunting is a measure for chronic hunger, wasting reflects an acute lack of energy. The interpretation of underweight is not entirely clear. Generally it is used as a summary indicator that takes account of both a low weight for age due to a very low weight for height as well as a low weight due to a low height for age.

As this paper will argue, the choice of underweight as the second measure for the hunger dimension of poverty is not very fortunate. On the one hand, there are doubts about the general construction and interpretation of underweight that make it not very suitable to be used as a summary indicator. On the other hand, and this will be the main focus of this paper, we can observe a bias in the development of underweight prevalence rates that is due to the large changes in the nutritional composition of diets in developing countries that are taking place. This so called 'nutrition transition' is characterized in large increases in the consumption of processed and semi-processed foods, that contain higher percentages of cheap fatty acids. Although this certainly means that total energy amounts taken up by children are increasing this should not be equalized with real improvements in their nutritional situation. Because of lacking vital micronutrients children might still suffer from severe growth retardations while having a weight for age that is not considerably below the growth and weight reference standard. Therefore, a secular reduction in weight based measures might show up that does not coincide with real improvements in the health of the affected children. In fact, as shown in Section 5, we can observe improvements in wasting and underweight rates in a number of countries that are not reflected in similar changes in stunting rates.

Therefore, it is argued that it would make sense to revise the undernutrition aspect of MDG I by using stunting rates or the also unbiased Composite Index of Anthropometric Failure (CIAF) instead of underweight rates. As the publication of the new multi-country reference standard by WHO is very likely to lead to a tracking of future progress using this new standard, a revision could take place during the adoption of the new reference standard.

The paper is structured as follows. Following a short description of the data in Section 2.2, Section 2.3 gives an overview over the differences in the incidence of undernutrition between the old and new reference standard and the advantages of the new reference standard. The subsequent Section 2.4 illustrates the changes in the nutrition status that are taking place in the developing world due to the progressing of the nutrition transition. Section 2.5 focuses on the empirical results and emphasizes the importance of having a closer look at the exact composition of undernutrition. Scrutinizing differences in the composition of undernutrition across different subgroups and over time shows that a strong bias is inherent in weight based measures.

2.2 Data

To get information on the prevalence and composition of undernutrition a sample of eleven countries from all developing regions is used. The data employed are nationally representative demographic and health surveys (DHS) surveys that provide information on anthropometric outcomes of children. To be able to illustrate changes in anthropometric outcomes two data sets for each country are used, bringing the total number of data sets two twenty-two (see Tab. 2.1).

The inclusion of countries was mainly driven by data availability. Only countries with at least two surveys were considered, with the surveys being spaced by at least 5 years and the latter survey being as recent as possible. Data availability for Asian countries was especially limited, since most surveys do not include any anthropometric information. Therefore India was used due to the well known high data quality as well as the huge number of observations.

Table 2.1: Data Sources: Demographic and Health Surveys (DHS)

Country	Year	Country	Year	Country	Year
Burkina Faso	1998/99	Colombia	1995	Tanzania	1996
Burkina Faso	2003	Colombia	2005	Tanzania	2004
Bolivia	1993/94	Egypt	1995	Uganda	1995
Bolivia	2003	Egypt	2003	Uganda	2000/01
Chad	1996/97	Ghana	1993	Zambia	1996
Chad	2003	Ghana	2003	Zambia	2001/02
Colombia	1995	India	1998/99		
Colombia	2005	India	1998/99		

The DHS datasets contain information on height, weight and age of all children below age 5 as well as the already computed Z-scores for the NCHS/WHO reference standard. Using a new version of the software ANTHRO published by WHO it is possible to use the anthropometric information to calculate Z-scores for the new WHO reference standard.

Besides the information on children, the DHS datasets contain a large set of other relevant covariates that play an important role in explaining child undernutrition, as for example the education of mothers or the area of residence. Unfortunately the surveys do not contain information on income or expenditure. Therefore an asset-based approach is used to define well-being (Sahn and Stifel, 2001).

In order to construct an asset index for DHS households, first, a set of household assets was identified, which were the ownership of a radio, TV, refrigerator, bicycle, motorized vehicle, floor material of housing, type of toilet, type of water source and some other assets depending on the country. Afterwards, these assets were aggregated into one single metric index for each household using the first component of principal component analysis, or, alternatively, the closely related factor analysis (see Filmer and Pritchett (2001) and Sahn and Stifel (2001)). In this case principal component analysis was used. Once the asset index is built, one can construct the cumulative distribution function of the asset index and, hence, households in the DHS can be classified into asset quintiles.

2.3   The new WHO Child Growth Standard

As is well known, there are a large number of limitations of the NCHS/WHO reference and these limitations have been documented by different authors (notably WHO Working Group on Infant Growth, 1994; de Onis and Yip, 1996; de Onis and Habicht, 1996). Between others the data used to construct the reference covering birth to two years of age were derived from a longitudinal study of children of European ancestry from a single community in the USA. Besides these children were measured only every three months, which is an inadequate way to describe the rapid and changing rate of growth in early infancy. Another aspect is that statistical methods have developed further in the last decades and are therefore better able to correctly model the pattern and variability of growth of children during their first five years.

As a consequence the WHO implemented the Multicentre Growth Reference Study (MGRS) which included children from six different countries: Brazil, Ghana, India, Norway, Oman and the USA. To make sure that only children were considered that are likely to have achieved their full genetic growth potential, only mothers from high socio-economic backgrounds were considered that engaged in fundamental health-promoting practices, namely breastfeeding and not smoking (de Onis et al., 2004). By selecting only privileged, healthy populations the study reduced the impact of environmental variation and is therefore very suitable to construct a truly international reference standard. [2]

These aspects make it very likely that the new WHO reference standard will be adopted as the main indicator to track the progress in reductions in child undernutrition according to MDG I. One first consequence will be that initial un-

---

[2]For a closer look at the appropriateness of using elites for the construction of a reference standard attention is drawn to Klasen and Moradi (2000).

dernutrition rates using the new WHO reference standard will decrease compared
to undernutrition rates using the old NCHS/WHO reference standard, when underweight is used as the only indicator. Tab. 2.2 shows the prevalence rates for
the four different anthropometric indicators using both reference standards for the
eleven countries considered in this study.

Table 2.2: Prevalence rates of undernutrition

(percentage)

Country	Reference	Stunting	Underweight	Wasting	CIAF
Burkina Faso 2003	NCHS/WHO	38.59	39.16	19.86	55.94
Burkina Faso 2003	WHO 2006	43.72	34.83	22.68	59.30
Bolivia 2003	NCHS/WHO	27.75	7.89	1.51	29.90
Bolivia 2003	WHO 2006	33.58	5.61	1.92	35.33
Chad 2004	NCHS/WHO	39.28	36.84	14.86	52.40
Chad 2004	WHO 2006	42.80	32.85	17.44	54.85
Cameroon 2004	NCHS/WHO	31.72	17.42	4.77	37.59
Cameroon 2004	WHO 2006	36.62	13.42	5.27	40.75
Colombia 2005	NCHS/WHO	12.06	7.63	1.67	15.40
Colombia 2005	WHO 2006	16.24	5.38	1.99	18.45
Egypt 2003	NCHS/WHO	15.78	8.62	3.68	20.76
Egypt 2003	WHO 2006	19.47	7.82	4.75	24.25
Ghana 2003	NCHS/WHO	30.90	23.43	7.69	40.17
Ghana 2003	WHO 2006	36.75	19.42	8.99	44.02
India 1998/99	NCHS/WHO	43.36	43.74	14.83	57.33
India 1998/99	WHO 2006	49.13	39.53	18.83	61.25
Tanzania 2004	NCHS/WHO	36.46	22.67	3.69	41.95
Tanzania 2004	WHO 2006	42.48	16.97	4.40	46.14
Uganda 2001/02	NCHS/WHO	37.88	21.50	3.93	42.57
Uganda 2001/02	WHO 2006	43.87	17.43	4.78	47.39
Zambia 2001/02	NCHS/WHO	47.55	28.64	4.84	53.39
Zambia 2001/02	WHO 2006	54.09	23.26	5.84	58.25

Source: DHS datasets; Own calculations.

Although the numbers in Tab. 2.2 show increases in stunting, wasting and
the Composite Index of Anthropometric Failure (CIAF), underweight rates fall in
all cases. This puzzling phenomenon will be discussed in more detail in Section
2.5. Besides these general trends, the numbers hide that changes in undernutrition
rates due to the adoption of the new reference standard are much more complex
than just a simple increases or decreases. This can be seen in Table 2.3 which is
a mobility matrix that shows that the composition of undernutrition changes considerably. Looking for example at the first row of Tab. 2.3 one can observe that
over 88% of children that were not malnourished according to the WHO/NCHS
reference standard are also not malnourished according to the new WHO reference standard. The remaining around 11% of the children are now considered as

only stunted (6.89%), stunted and underweight (0.64%), undernourished according to all three indicators (0.21%), only wasted (1.75%), wasted and underweight (0.88%) and only underweight (0.73%). But as mentioned before, the changes are not limited to increases in undernutrition rates, but a large number of individuals is now counted as not malnourished according to the new WHO reference standard that were categorized as malnourished using the NCHS/WHO reference standard. For example more than 16% of children that were only wasted according to the old reference standard are now considered as not malnourished and 39% of children that were only underweight according to the NCHS/WHO reference standard have z-scores above -2.0 according to the new standard. [3]

Table 2.3: Mobility matrix of NCHS/WHO to WHO reference standard (percentages)

	A	B	C	D	E	F	G
A - "Not malnourished"	88.88	6.89	0.64	0.21	1.75	0.88	0.73
B - "Only Stunted"	1.44	95.72	2.83	0.00	0.00	0.00	0.01
C - "Stunted and Underweight"	0.25	17.63	76.25	5.69	0.00	0.07	0.11
D - "All Indicators"	0.00	0.00	7.35	91.56	0.00	0.97	0.12
E - "Only Wasted"	16.42	0.00	0.00	0.03	71.30	12.25	0.00
F - "Wasted and Underweight"	5.02	0.00	1.11	10.04	11.47	68.47	3.89
G - "Only Underweight"	39.06	11.00	16.77	3.30	0.91	9.72	19.25

Note: *In each row the 100% of the respective category of the NCHS/WHO reference standard are divided into the same categories according to the new WHO reference standard. The percentages are generated from a pooled data set of all 22 data sets used in the present study.

These complex changes necessitate the complete revision of the nutrition aspect of MDG I using the new reference standard as basis for the measurement of progress in the reduction in undernutrition. This opportunity should be used to switch to stunting as alternative indicator, since all weight-based measures are inherently biased by the consequences of the Nutrition Transition as the following Section 2.4 will show.

2.4   The Nutrition Transition

Changes in diet and activity patterns are not limited to the developed countries but are rapidly taking place in the developing regions as well. For a large set of countries marked shifts in the structure of the diet have been documented (e.g. Kim et al. 2000, Monteiro et al. 1995, Popkin 1994, Popkin 1998). Major dietary

---

[3]For a closer description of the z-scores, the way they are generated and how one has to interpret them, attention is drawn to WHO (1995).

changes include large increases in the consumption of fat and added sugar in the diet and often a significant increase in animal food products. This is contrasted with a fall in total cereal intake and fiber. Although there is a great heterogeneity in the diet shifts, there seems to be a general shift to the higher fat Western diet, which is reflected by a large proportion of the population consuming over 30% of energy from fat. These diet and activity patterns are fueling the obesity epidemic that is also rapidly proceeding in the developing countries. As a consequence large increases in diet-related chronic diseases such as diabetes and cardiovascular diseases are discernable. In fact the WHO estimates that two thirds of deaths due to chronic disease worldwide now occur in developing countries and that obesity is a primary risk factor in this context (WHO 2004).

The nutrition transition and its related disease pattern might lead to the misconception that diets are moving entirely away from undernutrition toward problems of excess. Unfortunately the rapid increase in obesity does not come along with an equally rapid decrease in malnutrition or undernutrition. This could be the case due to the fact that not all individuals in a given society profit in the same way from increases in energy availability. During this transition, symptoms of under- and overnutrition logically coexist at the population level, with wealthier households exhibiting diseases of affluence including obesity, and poorer households exhibiting food insecurity and malnutrition. Recent work indicates that under- and overnutrition can even coexist in the same household (Doak et al. 2000, 2002; Monteiro et al. 1997). In fact the prevalence of stunted child-overweight mother pairs is not as seldom as one could assume, with the highest level being recorded for Egypt, where 14 percent of children live in stunted child-overweight mother pairs (Garrett and Ruel 2003). Besides Kandala et al. (2001) find a nonlinear influence of the BMI of the mother that might indicate that not only parental undernutrition, but also parental malnutrition might also have negative effects on the nutritional status of children. As is argued in the following the coexistence of under- and overweight in the same household is not due to a very unequal distribution of diets within households but the fact that increases in total energy intake do not coincide with equal increases in all vital micronutrients and, therefore, children might on average gain weight while still being malnourished.

It is therefore possible, that the nutrition transition will have two detrimental effects on policies concerning child undernutrition. On the one hand the emerging obesity epidemic might lead to the misconception that undernutrition is a phenomenon of the past. On the other hand using the 'wrong' indicator for undernutrition might also lead to wrong conclusions concerning the prevalence of undernutrition in developing countries. On the latter aspect will be the prime focus of this article. It is argued that the use of weight-based anthropometric measures is biased by the nutrition transition that leads to increases in the weight of children that do not necessarily reflect improvements in their nutritional status. They might still suffer from micronutrient malnutrition that will have severe long-term effects (Eckhardt 2006) and that is reflected in reduced long term growth of children. This micronutrient malnutrition can be accounted for when stunting is used as the anthropometric indicator for child undernutrition or alternatively the Composite Index of Anthropometric Failure (CIAF). The fact that such a bias is present in the underweight measure will be shown in the following sections.

Although it is argued that stunting is a much better measure for undernutrition than underweight or wasting, one has to keep in mind that a certain degree of overestimation is inherent in stunting, especially in comparison to a measure of average calorie availability like the FAO measure. This results from the fact that stunting measures the effective nutritional status and an inadequate access to calories is only one of the reasons why the growth of a child can falter. Other main reasons are frequent, prolonged and untreated illness that reduce the appetite and the absorption of energy in the body. Energy may also by diverted by intestinal parasites (Svedberg 2002).

A second aspect that has to be kept in mind is the fact that comparisons between countries and regions are made by using one general reference standard, i.e. using identical height and weight norms. It has been claimed that the genetic potential for growth in children is not the same for all regions (Bogin 1988, Davies 1988, Eveleth and Tanner 1990). Besides Klasen (2007) demonstrates that even minor differences of 1-3% in median height of children at age 5 between regions can lead to significant measurement biases, that result in an overestimation of the incidence of undernutrition in regions with a growth pattern of slightly lower growth. Still the consensus view seems to be that there are no or only very small genetic differences between populations in their growth and weight development between 0 and 5 years. This view is backed up by a variety of studies that showed that differences in growth and weight patterns between affluent groups of various countries are extremely similar (e.g. Graitcer and Gentry 1981, Ramalingaswami et al. 1996, WHO 1995, Bhandari et al. 2002).

It is important to keep in mind that these two confinements are not limited to stunting but general limitations of the three anthropometric measures. They can therefore not be used to favor any of these measures.

2.5 Results

The following section will first present some general aspects considering the construction of the underweight measure and especially point to the changes in prevalence rates between the old NCHS/WHO and the new WHO reference standard. Afterwards some empirical results with respect to the composition of undernutri-

tion and especially the composition over time will be discussed. All results are
based on own calculations using the aforementioned DHS surveys.

2.5.1   The theoretical composition of the underweight indicator

As mentioned before, undernutrition can be measured by three different anthropometric measures, namely stunting, wasting and underweight. The classical idea
of undernutrition, a low weight for height, is measured by wasting which is therefore a measure of immediate undernutrition. Contrary to that a long run supply of
insufficient amounts of energy will result in growth retardations which are measured by stunting (low height for age). Although it is well known that weight is
more sensitive than height to seasonal influences, but height generally more re-
sponsive than weight to improved food intake in the long term (WHO 1994), the
weight-based measure underweight (low weight for age) is used to track long term
changes in child undernutrition. This derives from the intention to take account of
both types of undernutrition, long-term as well as immediate.

Figure 2.1: Wasting/Stunting Combinations for Underweight of -2.0
(WHO reference standard)

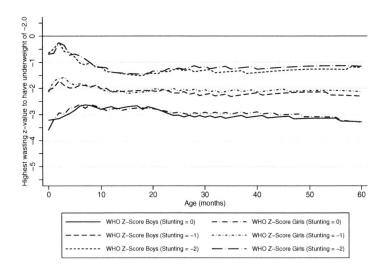

Source: WHO reference standard; own calculations.

Theoretically there are two reasons for a low weight for age. First, a value below 2 standard deviations of the reference standard can occur due to a very low weight for height. Second a underweight z-score of less than -2.0 can occur due to a very low height for age. Unfortunately underweight does not capture all individuals that are undernourished according to any of the other two measures. To demonstrate what children are really considered as 'underweight' different pairs of stunting and wasting z-scores are shown in Fig. 2.1 to 2.4 using both the NCHS/WHO and the WHO reference standard. These figures show that the relationship between stunting, wasting and underweight is rather complex. Besides the figures show that the underweight measures does not really capture what it is supposed to do.

Figure 2.2: Wasting/Stunting Combinations for Underweight of -2.0
(NCHS/WHO reference standard)

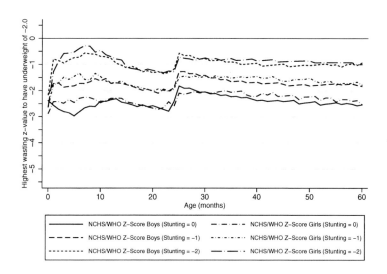

Source: NCHS/WHO reference standard; own calculations.

If underweight was really suitable as a summary indicator than for example every child that has a normal height for its age and a wasting z-score of below -2.0 would be counted as underweight. In fact as Fig. 2.1 and Fig. 2.2 show if it is assumed that a child has a height for age that corresponds to the new WHO reference standard (i.e. a stunting z-score of 0) has to have a wasting z-score of about -3 or below to have an underweight z-score of below -2.0. That means a boy or girl with normal height has to be severely wasted to be counted as underweight. When a child has a stunting z-score of -2 it still has to be slightly wasted and has to have a wasting z-score below -1 (depending on its exact age in months).

Using the old NCHS/WHO reference standard the relationship between stunting, wasting and underweight is even more complex, with a clear jump being discernable when the reference switches between length and height measures. This jump is not existent in the new WHO reference standard.

But what is even more important is the fact that the z-score requirements for wasting (for given stunting z-scores) are significantly lower in the NCHS/WHO reference standard than in the new WHO reference standard. A child with a height according to the old reference standard is counted as underweight, when it has an wasting z-score of about -2.5 or below. The differing z-score requirements between the two reference standards are easily observable in Tab. A.1 and A.2 in the Appendix B.

Figure 2.3: Stunting/Wasting Combinations for Underweight of -2.0

(Boys)

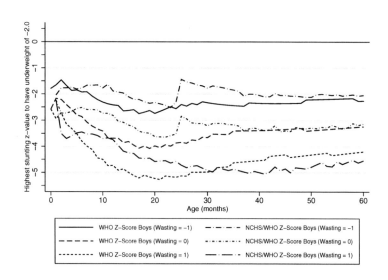

Source: WHO reference standard; own calculations.

Although it is not entirely clear how this shifts comes about, one possible reason could be that children with 'unhealthy weights for length/height', i.e. observations falling above +3SD and below -3SD of the sample median were excluded prior to constructing the WHO reference standard. For the cross-sectional sample the +2 SD cut-off was applied (WHO Multicentre Growth Reference Study Group 2006). The exclusion of this observations shifts the values of the weight standard downwards and therefore increases the weight shortfall requirements.

Figure 2.4: Stunting/Wasting Combinations for Underweight of -2.0

(Girls)

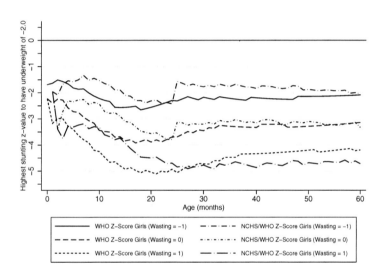

Source: NCHS/WHO reference standard; own calculations.

As Fig. 2.3 and 2.4 show, the requirements for stunting z-scores, given a 'normal' nutrition status according to wasting, are even more restrictive when the WHO reference standard is used. If boys or girls have a wasting z-score of 0, children have to have a stunting z-score of significantly below -3 to be counted as underweight. Only in the first eight month a stunting z-score between -2.5 and -3 is low enough to be also considered as underweight. If a child is mildly wasted (wasting z-score of -1) a child still has to be considerably stunted (stunting z-score of below -2) to be counted as underweight.

When looking at Fig. 2.3 and 2.4, we can again discover that the NCHS/WHO reference standard is not as restrictive as the WHO reference standard. The only exception is the scenario in which a wasting z-score of +1 is assumed. In this case only children with extremely low stunting z-scores do potentially fall in the group of underweight children. As Fig. **??** also shows, the NCHS/WHO curve is up to

the age of 26 months above and afterwards below the WHO curve. Fig. A.1 and
A.2 in the Appendix B show the curves for the old and new reference standard
separately. It is important to keep in mind, that increases in wasting z-scores are
very likely in the developing world due to the aforementioned nutrition transition.
The threshold be counted as underweight is therefore becoming more and more
restrictive.

As the preceding figures have shown, concentrating on a measure like underweight risks neglecting a large number of undernourished children. Although this
is also the case for the other two measures, - just as the concentration on any of
the other two indicators does. The only possibility to really capture all undernourished children is by using the Composite Index of Anthropometric Failure
(CIAF) proposed by Svedberg (2001) and modified by Nandy et al. (2005).[4] This
index indicates whether a child is undernourished according to any of the three
anthropometric indicators.

2.5.2   The empirical composition of the underweight indicator

Knowing the theoretical requirements for the underweight indicator it is of considerable interest to have a closer look at its actual composition. As Tab. 2.4
shows, more than 42% of children with an underweight z-score of below -2.0 exhibit stunting z-scores below -3.0. This already points to the strict requirements
for underweight, when undernutrition is limited to long-term undernutrition and
a child has a normal weight for its height. At the same time Tab. 2.4 shows that
some children that are considered neither as stunted nor wasted can at the same
time be indicated as underweight. In fact more than 12% of the 47,2222 children that are underweight according to the NCHS/WHO reference standard stem
from categories C and D in both indicators at the same time and are therefore neither considered as stunted nor wasted. It is therefore unclear whether it is really
appropriate to consider these children as undernourished.

The percentage of children that are only underweight and neither wasted nor
stunted is much lower when the new WHO reference standard is used (see Tab.
2.5). In this case only 4.84% of the remaining 42,424 children are at the same
time in categories C and D for both indicators. This reduction is entirely due to
the fact that the nutrition status has to be worse to get an underweight z-score of
below -2.0. This is demonstrated by the drop in the total number of underweight
children as well as by the fact that fraction of children that have severe growth
failures has increased to more than 54%.

---

[4]Nandy et al. (2005) that the CIAF consists of six subgroups contrary to the five groups
proposed by Svedberg (2002), with the last group being children that are undernourished according
to the underweight indicator only.

Table 2.4: Composition of group of underweight children
(using NCHS/WHO reference standard)

| | Wasting Z-Score | | | | | | |
Stunting Z-Score	A	B	C	D	E	F	Total
A - lower than -3.0	1.09	5.03	14.66	15.92	5.55	0.99	42.23
B - between -3.0 and -2.0	1.09	5.42	16.41	8.20	0.21	0.00	31.33
C - between -2.0 and -1.0	1.23	5.78	10.88	0.43	0.00	0.00	18.32
D - between -1.0 and 0.0	1.05	3.54	0.80	0.00	0.00	0.00	5.39
E - between 0.0 and 1.0	0.80	0.53	0.00	0.00	0.00	0.00	1.33
F - larger than 2.0	0.37	0.03	0.00	0.00	0.00	0.00	0.40
Total	5.64	20.32	42.75	24.54	5.76	0.99	100.00

Note: *Each cell denotes the percentage of all children with an underweight z-score of less than -2.0 that is in the respective category. The categories A-F are the same for wasting and stunting. In total there are 47,222 children with an underweight z-score of less than -2.0 according to the NCHS/WHO reference standard. *Source:* Pooled dataset of all 22 DHS datasets used in this study.

Table 2.5: Composition of group of underweight children
(using the new WHO reference standard)

| | Wasting Z-Score | | | | | | |
Stunting Z-Score	A	B	C	D	E	F	Total
A - lower than -3.0	4.17	7.04	15.36	18.60	6.90	2.15	54.21
B - between -3.0 and -2.0	2.69	5.46	12.90	4.51	0.24	0.00	25.81
C - between -2.0 and -1.0	2.81	5.52	4.62	0.16	0.00	0.00	13.11
D - between -1.0 and 0.0	2.38	2.12	0.06	0.00	0.00	0.00	4.56
E - between 0.0 and 1.0	1.39	0.05	0.00	0.00	0.00	0.00	1.44
F - larger than 2.0	0.87	0.00	0.00	0.00	0.00	0.00	0.87
Total	14.30	20.20	32.94	23.27	7.14	2.16	100.00

Note: *Each cell denotes the percentage of all children with an underweight z-score of less than -2.0 that is in the respective category. The categories A-F are the same for wasting and stunting. In total there are 42,424 children with an underweight z-score of less than -2.0 according to the new WHO reference standard. *Source:* Pooled dataset of all 22 DHS datasets used in this study.

Both the theoretical as well as the actual composition of the group of underweight children show that this indicator is not very suitable to be used as a summary indicator for undernutrition. In fact it is very doubtful whether it is an suitable indicator at all due to the difficulty in interpreting it and the inclusion of children that are not undernourished according to the other two better defined indicators. Besides it was shown, that the use of the new WHO reference standard will directly result in a decrease in the number of underweight children, although there are increases in stunting and wasting. Consequently it is by definition more difficult to be underweight and official figures will display decreases in the prevalence of undernutrition according to this indicator. It would therefore be highly recommendable to switch to an alternative indicator.

2.5.3 The Composition of Undernutrition across countries

When considering the choice of an alternative indicator it is very helpful to have a closer look at the exact composition of undernutrition across countries. As the data analysis of the 22 datasets in this study shows, this composition varies a lot between countries (see Fig. 2.5 - 2.7 below)[5]. Therefore concentrating on any of the three measures will not only neglect significant numbers of children that are undernourished according to a different indicator, but the general ranking of countries will also vary depending on which indicator is used.

Figure 2.5: Composition of undernutrition by countries (Group 1)

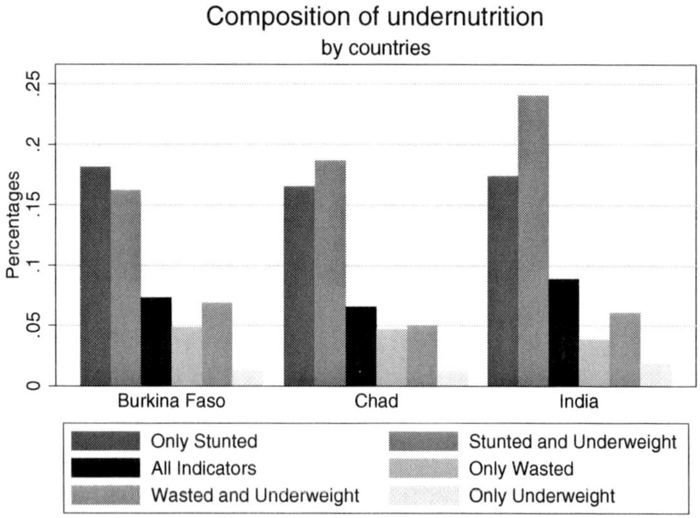

Source: DHS datasets; own calculations.

---

[5]It is important to note, that the only left out categories in all figures is the group of children that are not malnourished according to all indicators, that means that have higher Z-values than -2.0 for stunting, wasting and underweight. Besides the more recent dataset is used for all countries

By comparing the different general compositions of undernutrition it is possible to discern three different groups of countries. The first group (Fig. 2.5) are those countries where large percentages of the population have insufficient energy intakes (in this study Burkina Faso, Chad and India fall into this category). In these countries the lack of energy intake results not just in large numbers of stunted children but these growth retardations are so severe that a similar number of children is undernourished according to both stunting and underweight as is according to stunting only. A very significant number of children can also be found that are undernourished according to all three indicators. This shows an extremely bad nutritional status. Although already an adaptation of the growth process to the insufficient energy intake has taken place the energy amounts are still insufficient to generate a normal body composition.

Figure 2.6: Composition of undernutrition by countries (Group 2)

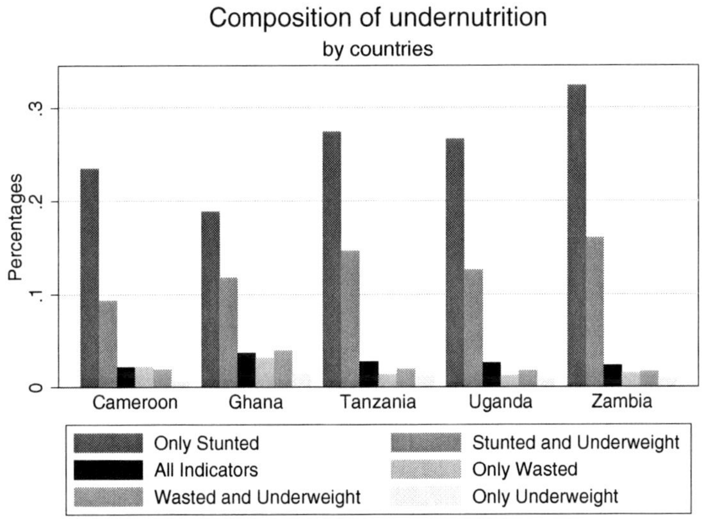

Source: DHS datasets; own calculations.

In the second group of countries (Fig. 2.6), i.e. Cameroon, Ghana, Tanzania, Uganda and Zambia, the prevalence of children that are only stunted is about twice as high as the prevalence of children that are undernourished according to both stunting and underweight. The prevalence of the other four categories is much lower than in the first group.

Finally, in the third group of countries (Fig. 2.7), i.e. Bolivia, Colombia and Egypt, undernutrition is almost completely confined to stunting. The ratio of stunting to stunting and underweight is even higher and the number of children with Z-values of lower than -2.0 according to all three indicators is almost negligible.

Figure 2.7: Composition of undernutrition by countries (Group 3)

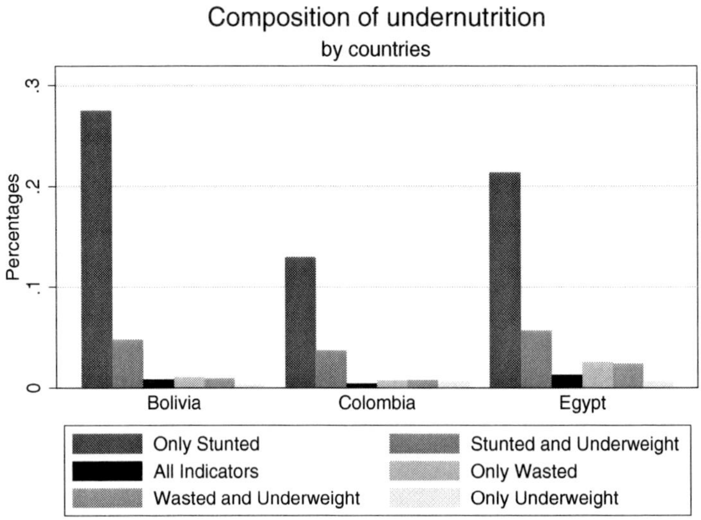

Source: DHS datasets; own calculations.

As a comparison of the three general groups shows, stunting is the most persistent measure, displaying the highest rates in the last group as well as the lowest improvements between groups. This fact can also be seen, when we compare different subgroups for children in any given country.

2.5.4   Composition of Undernutrition across subgroups

Interestingly enough the general country patterns are very consistent over different subcategories. A good way of showing this is by comparing the composition of

undernutrition across different wealth groups. Since no expenditure or income
data are available in the DHS datasets, an asset-based approach is used to define
wealth (Sahn and Stifel, 2001).

Figure 2.8: Composition of undernutrition in India by asset index quintiles

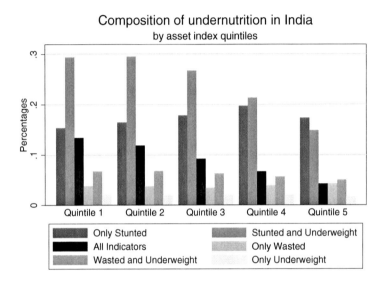

Source: DHS dataset (India 1998/99); own calculations.

The composition of undernutrition across asset index quintiles shows a strong
decrease in the categories 'Stunted and Underweight' and 'All Indicators' whereas
prevalence rates in the other categories remain almost constant. Therefore improvements between wealth categories are almost entirely due to differences in
weight-based measures in the case of India. This tendency is found in many of the
other countries as well, one other example being Burkina Faso (see Fig. A.3 Appendix B. Another case shown in the appendix is Bolivia, where improvements in
stunting are visible, but it is also obvious that stunting is by far the most persistent
indicator (see Fig. A.4).

Another possible way to demonstrate what effects changes in dietary intakes
will have on the prevalence rates and composition of undernutrition is by comparing different subcategories of the nutrition status of the mother. Although an
increase in the BMI of a mother, especially over 25, does not necessarily reflect

an increase in well-being it still leads to reductions in the prevalence rates of all categories that include the two weight-based measures. In fact an BMI of 25 is generally used as threshold value to differentiate between normal weight and overweight (with a BMI of over 30 indicating that the respective person is obese). Being overweight has considerable negative effects of it's own on the health of the mother and should therefore influence children negatively as well. As a consequence it is not clear from a theoretical perspective why the prevalence rates of undernutrition of children of overweight mothers should be lower than the prevalence rates of children of mothers with normal weight. But as the following Fig. 2.9 shows, prevalence rates of undernutrition seem to be lower in the subcategory of overweight mothers than in the subcategory of mothers with normal weight.

Figure 2.9: Composition of undernutrition in Uganda by nutrition status of mother

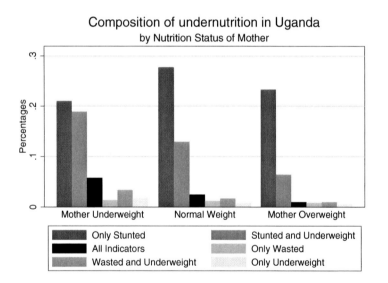

Source: DHS dataset (Uganda 2000/01); own calculations.
Notes: Underweight is defined as a BMI below 18.5, normal weight as a BMI between 18,5 and 25 and overweight as a BMI above 25.

The general findings for Uganda are representative for all countries that were looked at in the present study and can also be seen in the figures for Chad and India (see Fig. A.5 and A.6 in Appendix B). Namely increases in the BMI of the mother do not lead to a universal decline in the prevalence rates of childhood undernutrition. On the contrary these improvements are mainly limited to the weight-based measures and stunting remains almost unaffected.

The observed patterns are not consistent with an explanation that increases in the BMI of mothers are a proxy for improvements in the wealth of households and therefore lead to general improvements in child anthropometry. The pattern is more consistent with a theory that states that the BMI of the mother is a good proxy for the dietary composition of a household. A higher BMI is consequently an indicator for a diet in the household that is rich in cheap fatty acids. A higher weight or BMI of the mother is therefore correlated with a higher weight of the child which does not necessarily reflect a better nutritional status. As mentioned before, higher amounts of energy from foods do not necessarily coincide with sufficient amounts of vital micronutrients.

Restrictively it has to be stated that the BMI of the mother is susceptible to a number of biases. For example, a bad nutritional status of the mother during her childhood and the resulting growth retardations can increase the likelihood of being overweight according to the BMI because of the small body height.

2.5.5 Changes in Undernutrition over Time

Probably the clearest and best way to show how focusing on the 'wrong' indicator for undernutrition will lead to a considerable bias in measurement is by comparing prevalence rates over time. Here, the secular downward trend in the prevalence of weight-based undernutrition, that is not reflected in a similar improvement in stunting or the Composite Index of Anthropometric Failure, is extremely obvious.

Looking at the following Tab. 2.6, it is discernable that changes over time are not the same for all three indicators of undernutrition. In fact, the magnitude of changes does not only differ between stunting, wasting and underweight but also the direction of change differs.

On the one hand, we can observe decreases in all three measures in Colombia, Egypt, India and Tanzania, no significant changes in any measure are observable in Chad and increases in all three measures are found in Burkina Faso and Zambia. On the other hand, the directions of change differ in Bolivia, Cameroon, Ghana and Uganda. In all these countries reductions in wasting and underweight took place, while stunting increased.

It is clear that decreases in weight-based anthropometric measures that come along with increases in stunting are only very extreme examples. Fortunately in most countries the prevalence of undernutrition was reduced according to all measures. But even in these countries the magnitude of the change is not the same for all three anthropometric indicators. A stronger decrease in weight-based measures compared to stunting are again observable when we compare the two

Table 2.6: Anthropometric indicators over time
(WHO 2006 reference standard)

Survey (Year)	Stunting	Underweight	Wasting	CIAF
Differing Directions				
Bolivia (1993/94)	33.4%	12.2%	6.1 %	38.1%
Bolivia (2003)	33.7%	5.5%	1.9%	35.4%
Cameroon (1998)	34.0%	16.1%	8.0%	39.6%
Cameroon (2003)	36.6%	13.3%	5.5%	40.9%
Ghana (1993)	33.0%	24.7%	14.6%	44.2%
Ghana (2003)	36.7%	19.4%	9.0%	44.0%
Uganda (1995)	41.5%	19.3%	6.8%	45.9%
Uganda (2000/01)	43.8%	17.2%	4.8%	47.3%
Same Directions				
Burkina Faso (1998/99)	43.5%	31.7%	15.4%	54.6%
Burkina Faso (2003)	43.6%	34.5%	22.7%	59.4%
Chad (1996/97)	43.3%	32.4%	16.2%	53.7%
Chad (2004)	42.6%	32.3%	17.4%	54.9%
Colombia (1995)	19.8%	6.2%	1.7%	21.7%
Colombia (2005)	16.3%	5.3%	2.0%	18.5%
Egypt (1995)	34.7%	11.8%	7.3%	40.9%
Egypt (2003)	19.7%	7.7%	4.8%	24.5%
India (1992/93)	54.1%	43.8%	19.0%	65.7%
India (1998/99)	48.9%	38.8%	18.7%	61.1%
Tanzania (1996)	50.1%	26.6%	8.7%	56.0%
Tanzania (2004)	42.6%	16.9%	4.4%	46.3%
Zambia (1996)	50.2%	20.1%	5.4%	54.2%
Zambia (2001/02)	53.8%	22.9%	6.0%	58.2%

Note: *Children are considered as wasted, stunted or underweight if the respective z-scores are below -2 standard deviation from the median of the reference category.

surveys for each country. Below the development over time is shown for India and Tanzania in Fig. 2.10.

Figure 2.10: Composition of undernutrition in India and Tanzania by survey year

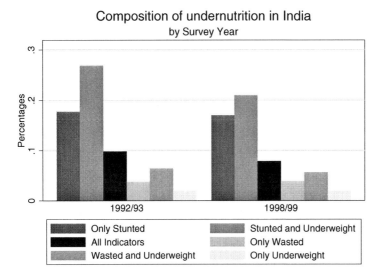

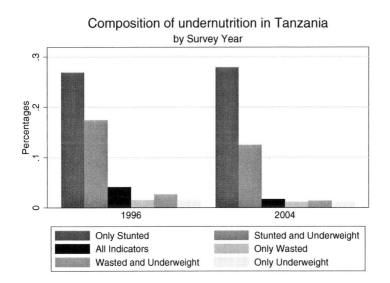

Source: DHS datasets; own calculations.

The analysis of changes over time confirms therefore the results of the analysis of the general composition of undernutrition and the analysis of different subgroups. In all cases can be shown that the two weight-based show stronger reductions than stunting, which is by far the most persistent indicator of child undernutrition with the lowest rates in improvement. This is important to keep in mind because if the falling prevalence rates in the two weight-based measures where really due to considerable improvements in the nutrition status of children than stunting rates would fall in a similar manner. Since this is not the case, it is reasonable to assume that weight increases due to changes in dietary composition play an important role in these changes. These weight gains should not be counted as improvements per se and it would therefore make sense to use stunting instead of underweight as the indicator of choice.

2.6 Conclusion

As the preceding chapters have demonstrated it is very helpful to have a closer look at the exact composition of undernutrition. Although the general pattern is very durable in each country across subgroups there are large differences between countries that will lead to different country rankings depending on which indicator is used.

Besides this general aspect, it was argued that especially the use of underweight as the measure of choice to track the progress in the fight against undernutrition is highly problematic. Due to the way this indicator is defined, children either have to be extremely undernourished according to one indicator or have to be moderately undernourished according to both indicators. Consequently a large number of children are not considered as underweight that are significantly stunted or wasted. And some children are considered as underweight that are neither stunted nor wasted. Since the interpretation of the underweight indicator on its own is not very straightforward, there are considerable doubts whether it is a useful indicator at all.

Further it was demonstrated that the use of the new WHO reference standard alone results in significant reductions in the prevalence of underweight, although the other two indicators show increases. Adding to this reduction is the general downward trend in all weight based measures, such as underweight and wasting, that is due to changes in the nutritional composition of diets in developing countries. This secular reduction does not necessarily coincide with real improvements in the health of the affected children due to still lacking micronutrients. This bias makes the interpretation of reductions in the prevalence rates of undernutrition even more problematic and could lead to wrong conclusions concerning the fulfillment of the undernutrition aspect of MDG I.

While on a scientific level it is very useful to have a closer look at the exact composition of undernutrition, it is acknowledged at the same time, that the necessity exists on a political level to have a single indicator to count the number of undernourished persons. Consequently the opportunity of the introduction of the new WHO reference standard should be used to switch to stunting or the Composite Index of Anthropometric Failure (CIAF) instead of underweight as the indicator to measure progress in the field of undernutrition. Both measures do not suffer from biases that are introduced due to the nutrition transition that is taking place in the developing countries and are much easier to interpret.

Essay 3

A Regional Puzzle of Child Mortality and Undernutrition

Abstract: While undernutrition among children is very pervasive both in Sub-Saharan Africa and South Asia, child mortality is rather low in South Asia. In contrast to that, Sub-Saharan African countries suffer by far the worst from high rates of child mortality. This different pattern of child mortality and undernutrition in both regions is well known, but approaches using aggregated macro-data have not been able to explain it appropriately. In this paper, we analyze the determinants of child mortality as well as child undernutrition based on DHS data sets for a sample of five developing countries in South Asia and Sub-Saharan Africa. We investigate the effects of individual, household, and cluster socio-economic characteristics using a multilevel model approach and examine their respective influences on both phenomena. The results show significant differences in outcomes of child mortality and undernutrition and in their respective determinants between the two regions and between countries. Whereas the access to health infrastructure is more important for child mortality than for undernutrition, the nutritional status of the mother, which is worse in South Asia than in Sub-Saharan Africa, has a much higher impact on child undernutrition than on child mortality.

based on joint work with Kenneth Harttgen.

3.1   Introduction

3.1.1   Child Mortality and Undernutrition

Despite the overall decline in the prevalence of undernutrition and child mortality in developing countries, both phenomena are still at unacceptably high levels and, therefore, remain big challenges in the fight against lacking capabilities and reaching the MDGs. Concerning the childrens' anthropometric failure, the WHO (2002) estimated that almost 27 percent (168 million) of children under five years of age are underweight. And looking at the threat of child mortality, nearly 11 million children died in the year 2003 before reaching the age of five. Around 98 percent of the deaths occur in developing countries (UN, 2005). Several papers have studied the socio-economic determinants of child mortality and undernutrition. Examples for empirical studies of child mortality are Subbaro and Rany (1995), Pritchett and Summers (1996), Ssewanyana and Younger (2004), and for undernutrition Gillespie et al (1996), Osmani (1997), and more recently Smith and Haddad (2000). As stated in numerous studies in this field, one of the major causes of child mortality is undernutrition itself. Most studies cite this result by referring to a study by Pelletier et al. (1995), which finds that more than 50 percent of child mortality is attributable to mild, moderate, and severe undernutrition. In addition, a study of Pelletier et al. (2002) measures the effect of malnutrition on changes in child mortality for 59 developing countries using aggregate longitudinal data from 1966 to 1996, finding that reducing malnutrition by 5 percent could reduce under-five child mortality by 30 percent. Although, intuitively it seems to be clear that being malnourished increases the risk of child mortality, considerable doubts concerning the closeness of the relationship exist.

3.1.2   The South Asia - Sub-Saharan Africa Enigma

Assuming a close relationship between child mortality and undernutrition, two glaring puzzles exist when the two regions of South Asia and Sub-Saharan Africa are compared. The first puzzle is the so called South Asian Enigma. The anthropometric outcomes are considerably better in Sub-Saharan Africa than in South Asia. Almost half of the children in South Asia are malnourished. Compared to Sub-Saharan Africa the anthropometric shortfall is almost 70 percent higher in South Asia (WHO, 2005), despite higher per capita calorie availability and better provision of health care, water, and sanitation (Ramalingaswami et al., 1996; Osmani, 1997; Svedberg, 2002). The second puzzle concerns the existing child mortality reversals between these two regions (Svedberg, 2000; Klasen, 2003, 2007). In contrast to the severe anthropometric failure in South Asia, Sub-Saharan African countries suffer by far the worst from high rates of child mortality. In Sub-Saharan

Africa, 174 children out of 1000 die before reaching the age of five, while 97 die in South Asia (UNICEF, 2004). Together, these two puzzles can then be defined as the South Asia - Sub-Saharan Africa Enigma of anthropometric failure and mortality reversals.

Various possible explanations for the Enigma exists. First, the level of income poverty is a obvious and major cause both for child mortality and undernutrition, but this cannot explain the regional differences as the average incidence of poverty is quite similar in the two regions. Second, the high magnitude of undernutrition is a result of how undernutrition is measured. For example, Klasen (2003, 2007) argues that the US-based reference standard for international comparison of undernutrition proposed by the WHO (1995) leads to an overestimation of undernutrition in South Asia. This overestimation could be due to different genetic potential in growth between the population in these two regions. The high level of undernutrition in South Asia might then appear because of genetic differences in height and weight, i.e. that children in South Asia are genetically shorter and/or lighter compared to the reference population and are, therefore, spuriously considered as malnourished. But even if this is the case, this could explain only a part of the large differences in the anthropometric outcomes between South Asia and Sub-Saharan Africa. However, also the use of the new reference standard by the WHO (WHO, 2006) that is based on child growth data from six different developed and developing countries[1] that takes explicitly into account the growth potential of children by selecting children from well-doing households, has not been able to solve the Enigma. In particular, using the new reference standard only leads to an upward shift in the level of anthropometric measures compared to the old reference standard, but it does not provide any changes in the ratio of the outcomes of anthropometric measures between South Asia and Sub-Saharan Africa (see also Klasen, 2007). Besides, several authors have demonstrated evidence that no real genetic differences exist between childrens' growth paths below the age of five in South Asia (see e.g. Gopalan, 1992; Eveleth and Tanner, 1990; Svedberg, 2000; Svedberg, 2002), which suggests that these differences are caused by other factors, although a final conclusion concerning the influence of genetic factors on childrens' growth paths is not yet possible. Third, the relative higher rates of child mortality in Sub-Saharan Africa than in South Asia can partly be explained through the fact that Sub-Saharan Africa is much more affected by diseases, among other things also due to climatic reasons. In addition, the high incidence of HIV/AIDS and Malaria can potentially explain a part of the Enigma, but a further assessment of this effect is strongly constraint by data availability. Fourth, the primary health care provision and other public services are possible

---

[1]Brazil, Oman, Ghana, India, USA, and Norway. For more information on the new reference standard see Chapter 2.

explanations, which is less adequately provided in Sub-Saharan Africa (Svedberg, 1999; Ramalingaswami et al., 1996). Fifth, a further explanation is that the same determinants of child mortality and undernutrition may have different impacts in the two regions or that both phenomena are not as closely related as generally assumed (see e.g. Seckler, 1982; Messer, 1986).[2]

Explaining the different relationships of child mortality and undernutrition between these two forms of deprivation within a country and also between countries and regions has important policy implications, as it supports a much more detailed assessment of required policy interventions to fight child mortality and undernutrition in order to reach the MDGs. But approaches using aggregated macro-data have not been able to explain this regional puzzle appropriately. So far, we find no attempts to explain the South Asia - Sub-Saharan Africa Enigma from a microeconomic perspective that have analyzed the socio-economic determinants simultaneously for child mortality and undernutrition with the focus on their differences and similarities using micro-data.

This paper analyzes the regional puzzle of child mortality and undernutrition between South Asia and Sub-Saharan Africa. The aim of the paper is helping to explain the South Asia - Sub-Saharan Africa Enigma using micro-data. To achieve this, we address three main issues concerning the explanation of the Enigma. First, we analyze the relationship between child mortality and undernutrition. We simultaneously try to find socio-economic determinants that affect child mortality and undernutrition. In particular, we try to find out, which determinants drive undernutrition as well as child mortality in a similar way and what factors have differing effects on both phenomena. Identifying determinants that drive both phenomena in a different way can than help to explain the Enigma. Second, analyzing the determinants of child mortality and undernutrition, we concentrate also on region-specific differences both in the outcomes and determinants of both phenomena. This allows us to identify major differences that drives the puzzle of child mortality and undernutrition in the two regions. Third, we also focuss on country-specific differences. Especially, if countries differ in the outcomes of socio-economic characteristics that have different impacts on child mortality and undernutrition. In addition to these three issues, we argue that socio-economic characteristics at the community level (e.g. infrastructure) play an important role both for child mortality and undernutrition, but standard regression models do not allow to incorporate these higher-level information appropriately. Therefore, in contrast to most cross-country studies that investigate the determinants of child mortality and undernutrition, we introduce the methodology of multilevel mod-

---

[2]In particular, the assumed small relationship between child mortality and undernutrition goes back to the so-called 'small but healthy' hypothesis, which claims that populations adapt to different physical and socio-economic environments and that individuals can adapt to lower levels of energy and protein intakes without suffering from functional deteriorations (Seckler, 1982).

elling into our analysis that explicitly takes into account the hierarchical structure of the Demographic and Health Survey (DHS) data sets. This will also help to provide information about differences in the outcome variables due to differences in community characteristics, especially about the provision of infrastructure service. We investigate the effects of individual, household, and cluster socio-economic characteristics on anthropometric shortfalls and child mortality to examine their respective influences and relationships on both phenomena and to capture both within and between community effects in a single model. For the empirical analysis we use several nationally representative DHS data for a sample of five developing countries in South Asia and Sub-Saharan Africa.

The results show determinants of child mortality and undernutrition that differ significantly from each other. Access to health infrastructure is more important for child mortality, whereas individual characteristics like wealth and educational and nutritional characteristics of mothers play a larger role for anthropometric shortfalls. Although very similar patterns in the determinants of each phenomenon are discernable, we find large differences in the magnitude of the coefficients. However, regressions using a combined data set including all five countries and dummies for the two regions show that there are still significant differences between the two regions that remain unexplained. Both region dummies as well as numerous interaction effects are significant. Therefore, given the underlying data and the proposed methodology, the South Asia - Sub-Saharan Africa Enigma cannot be fully solved by different levels in access to health facilities, education, wealth, and status of women alone. The results suggest that unobserved characteristics (e.g. HIV/AIDS) on the one hand and the measurement of undernutrition on the other hand might also play an important role to explain the Enigma.

The paper is structured as follows. After the given problem statement and an overview about the existing literature on measuring child mortality and child undernutrition and the differences in their outcomes in South Asia and Sub-Saharan Africa, Section 3.2 explains the empirical method of multilevel models and specifies our model. Section 3.3 presents the data sources. In Section 3.3.2, first descriptive statistics show the different patterns of child mortality and undernutrition within and between the analyzed countries. Second, in Section 3.3.3, we provide estimation results of the multilevel analysis. Third and finally, we simulate changes in the outcome variables for changes in selected covariates. Section 3.4 concludes.

3.2 Methodology

3.2.1 Multilevel Analysis

Many population based household surveys in economics have a clustered or hierarchical data structure, where a hierarchy consists of units grouped at different levels. For instance, individuals (level 1) are nested within households (level 2), households are nested within communities (level 3), and communities are nested within states and countries. Standard regression models have problems dealing with the hierarchical data structure, even if we only include variables at level one (i.e. the child level), since they assume independent and normally distributed errors with a constant variance. But analyzing variables from different levels without taking into account the hierarchical data structure might lead to misleading estimation results, because one faces the problem of heteroscedasticity. The individual observations in hierarchical data structure are not completely independent, and the results of the analysis can be affected by this clustered structure of the underlying data. To put it differently, households in the same community are more homogenous than households in different communities. In particular, in the case of child undernutrition this means that the anthropometric outcomes in different communities might be independent from each other, but that outcomes within a community are not independent, especially when children live in the same household. This leads to a violation of the assumption of independent errors, i.e. the assumption of homoscedasticity, which has consequences for the estimation results. The estimated coefficients are unbiased but not efficient because the standard errors are negatively biased, which leads to misleading significance inference. What is typically done in the empirical literature is to regress an independent variable at the lowest level on a set of explanatory variables available for any other level by disaggregating all higher level variables to the individual level. This is done, for example, by assigning each individual in the same community the same value of the community variable. But this leads to the problem of inefficient estimation results mentioned before.[3]

In this analysis, we want to study whether mortality rates and undernutrition rates differ between several individual and household characteristics that vary from community to community, on the basis of clustered household surveys. Furthermore, we are concerned with understanding the factors associated with variations between regions, countries, and within a country between communities. This means that we want to analyze the impact of community characteristics on the two outcome variables, e.g. the access to health facilities, and how much of the

---

[3]One can also think of aggregating the variables of the individual level to a higher level and do the analysis on the higher level. However, in many cases this leads to a loss of the within-group information we are interested in.

between-community variation is explained by community explanatory variables. Instead of relying upon the use of standard regression models, a more adequate way to take into account the hierarchical data structure is the methodology of multilevel modeling. A multilevel model is concerned with the analysis of the relationship between variables that are measured at different hierarchical levels (Hox, 2002). The aim of a multilevel model is to take explicitly into account this data structure and to determine the direct effect of the individual and the group explanatory variables. Methodological work on analyzing multilevel models was done, for instance, by Bryk and Raudenbush (1992), Goldstein (1999, 1987), and more recently by Hox (2002), who gives an illustrative introduction to multilevel models with an application to educational data.[4]

Multilevel models correct for the bias in the parameter estimates resulting from the clustered data structure, because in a multilevel model each level is represented by it own sub-model, which expresses the relationship among explanatory variables within that level. This possibility leads to several advantages using multilevel modelling. First, it provides statistically efficient estimates of the regression coefficients by providing correct standard errors, confidence intervals, and significance tests (Goldstein, 1999). Second, cross-level effects and cross-level interactions, i.e. the relationship of variables at different levels, can be analyzed. This means, measuring covariates at each level provides the possibility to analyze the extent to which differences in child mortality and undernutrition between communities are due to community factors like access to health facilities or due to factors at the individual level like gender. Third, estimates of the variances and covariances at each level of the model allows to decompose the total variance in the outcome variable into fractions for each level. In the so-called variance component models, the error term is divided into two parts, the group component and the individual component. This allows the assessment of the variation that is due to differences at the group-level and due to differences at the individual level.[5]

---

[4]The first multilevel analysis in social sciences was done by Aitkin et al. (1981). He analyzed the impact of the teaching style on progress in reading capabilities of children in primary schools in Great Britain using traditional multiple regression techniques shown by Bennett (1976). When the data is analyzed only with the individual children as the units of the analysis without recognizing that they are groups within classes, the results were statistically significant. When the grouping of children in classes is taken into account, then the significant differences between teaching styles found before disappear.

[5]For instance, Pebley et al. (1996) investigate the receipt of vaccinations of children in Guatemala with variables at the individual, at the household, and at the community level. When controlling for the observed variables, they found that the variance due to households is five times higher than due to communities.

3.2.2   The Basic Multilevel Model

In a multilevel model, the dependent variable is located at the lowest level, in our case the individual (child) level. Following Hox (2002), the basic multilevel model with two different levels can be described as follows. Suppose that we have $j = 1, ..., J$ level 2 units (i.e. communities), where there are $i = 1, ..., n_j$ level 1 units (i.e. children). Then, we can speak of child i being nested within community j. To analyze the outcome variable, we can set up the regression equation as follows:

$$Y_{ij} = \beta_{0j} + \beta_{1j} X_{ij} + e_{ij} \qquad (3.1)$$

with β_0 as the intercept and β_1 as the slope, defined as the expected change in the dependent variable with an increase in the individual variable X of one unit.[6] The difference to standard regression models is that equation 3.1 contains two subscripts, one referring to the individual i and one to the community level j. The clustered data structure and the within- and between-community variations are now taken into account by assuming that each community has a different intercept β_{0j} and a different slope β_{1j}. Then, the explanatory variables at the second level Z can be introduced into the model. For this, the coefficients β_{0j} and β_{1j} are themselves given in a regression model as dependent variables via two regression equations with the level two variables as the independent explanatory variables:

$$\beta_{0j} = \gamma_{00} + \gamma_{01} Z_j + u_{0j} \qquad (3.2)$$

$$\beta_{1j} = \gamma_{10} + \gamma_{11} Z_j + u_{1j}. \qquad (3.3)$$

Equations 3.2 and 3.3 explain the variations between communities, because the intercept β_{0j} and the slope β_{1j} depend on the community variables in community j. For example, Equation 3.2 predicts the average anthropometric outcome of the child at the level 2 variable Z in community j. Equation 3.3 states that the slope β_{1j} between the anthropometric outcome (Y) and level-1 variable (X), i.e. gender, depends on the level-2 variable (Z), i.e. access to health. The error terms u_{0j} and u_{1j} are level-2 residuals.[7]

The combined model can now be expressed by one single regression equation by substituting Equations 3.2 and 3.3 into Equation 3.1:

$$Y_{ij} = \gamma_{00} + \gamma_{10} X_{ij} + \gamma_{01} Z_j + \gamma_{11} X_{ij} Z_j + (u_{1j} X_{ij} + u_{0j} + e_{ij}). \qquad (3.4)$$

---

[6]We assume that the errors e_{ij} have a mean of zero so that $E(e_{ij}) = 0$ and a variance $var(e_{ij}) = \sigma_e^2$ so that $e_{ij} \sim N(0, \sigma_e^2)$.

[7]The residuals u_{0j} and u_{1j} are also assumed to have mean of zero so that $E(u_{oj}) = E(u_{1j}) = 0$. It is also assumed that the variance is defined as $var(u_{oj}) = \sigma_{u_0}^2$, $var(u_{1j}) = \sigma_{u_1}^2$, and the covariance as $cov(u_{oj}, u_{1j}) = \sigma_{u_{01}}$. A positive value of the covariance between β_0 and β_1 indicates that communities with high means tend also to have positive slopes.

In Equation 3.4, the first part can be defined as the deterministic part referring to the fixed coefficients, which means that coefficients do not vary across level. The part of Equation 3.4 expressed in parentheses can be defined as the stochastic part, containing the random error terms. The term $X_{ij}Z_j$ is an interaction term analyzing the cross-level interaction.[8]

The stochastic part in Equation 3.4 again demonstrates the problem of dependent errors. In contrast to standard ordinary least squares (OLS) regression, the error term in 3.4 contains one individual component e_{ij} and a group or community component $u_{0j} + u_{1j}X_{ij}$. The individual error component e_{ij} is independent across all individuals. In contrast, the community level errors u_{0j} and u_{1j} are independent between communities, but dependent within each community, because the components are the same for every child i in community j. These dependencies lead to unequal variances of the error terms, which results into heteroscedasticity, because $u_{0j} + u_{1j}X_{ij}$ depend on u_{0j} and u_{1j}, which vary across communities, and on X_{ij}, which vary across children.

3.2.3 Model Specification

In our multilevel analysis, we set up a 2-level model to identify, which socio-economic characteristics determine child mortality and undernutrition and to explain the South Asia - Sub-Saharan Africa Enigma. Level 1 includes both individual and household variables, level 2 is the cluster level. We do not differentiate between the individual (child) level and the household level, because there are no real differences between individual and the household information, since there are only a very few households with more than three young children in the data.[9]

The empirical analysis proceeds in 6 basic steps. First, we run several regression model types to get a benchmark for our two outcome variables and to explain the differences between the multilevel approach and standard regression models. For child mortality, we run a logit regression. For stunting, we also run a logit regression on a dummy whether the child is stunted and an OLS regression on the stunting z-scores.[10] Second, to build up the multilevel model, we start by including all explanatory variables of level 1 into the model, which means that the

---

[8]As OLS estimations techniques are inappropriate to deal with the within level-2 dependencies, the multilevel analysis is based on an iterative maximum likelihood estimation (Mason et al., 1983; Goldstein, 1987; Bryk and Raudenbsuh, 1992). An advantage of the maximum likelihood method is that it provides estimates that are asymptotically efficient and consistent (for a detailed description of maximum likelihood estimation technique, see e.g. Eliason (1993)).

[9]When setting up a multilevel model, Maas and Hox (2004) suggest a sample size for the second level of more than 50.

[10]See Section 3.3.1 below for a description of the dependent and independent variables.

variance component of the slopes is fixed to zero.[11] This model serves as a benchmark for the two variance components. Third, we set up the full model by adding the explanatory variables of the community level. Comparing this model with the model in step 3 allows us to investigate whether and to what extent the between-community variation in child mortality and child undernutrition is explained by community characteristics.

For a meaningful interpretation of the intercept, we center each explanatory variable around the grand mean by subtracting the grand mean from each variable.[12] Thus, Equation 3.4 becomes:

$$Y_{ij} = \gamma_{00} + \gamma_{10}(X_{ij} - \bar{X}) + \gamma_{01}(Z_{qj} - \bar{Z}) + \gamma_{11}(X_{ij} - \bar{X})(Z_j - \bar{Z})$$

$$+ [u_{1j}(X_{ij} - \bar{X}) + u_{0j} + e_{ij}]. \tag{3.5}$$

Following the multilevel analysis, in step five, we merge all country data sets to one global data set and run the multilevel regression again testing for specific country and region fixed effects for each country in the sample to identify differences in the effects of the explanatory variables on child mortality and undernutrition between countries in South Asia and Sub-Saharan Africa. Here, the independent variables enter into the regression as the mean values per cluster to explicitly take into account regional differences within countries. In addition, we include a Sub-Saharan Africa dummy to capture regional differences and to check whether the Enigma still persists, when controlling four demographic and socio-economic characteristics. Furthermore, the region dummy is also interacted with all explanatory variables at each level. Finally, in step six, the analysis is extended by constructing a simulation of several scenarios for child mortality and undernutrition. Here, we compare changes in the outcome variables for potential changes in specific covariates to check whether the differences in the outcomes of the socio-economic characteristics between the two regions can help to explain the Enigma.

---

[11]In particular, we assume that $u_{1j} = 0$.

[12]The reason of centering the explanatory variables is the interpretation of the intercept β_0. As it is defined as the expected value of the outcome variable when all explanatory variables have a value of zero, we face the problem that this would be misleading for some dummy variables because they are coded as 1 and 0. If we center the variables around their grand mean, the intercept becomes the expected value of the outcome variable, when all variables have their mean value.

3.3 Empirical Analysis

3.3.1 Data Description

To obtain possible explanations about the regional differences in child mortality and undernutrition between South Asia and Sub-Saharan Africa, we analyze a sample of five countries from these regions. We use nationally representative DHS data that provide information on anthropometric outcomes of children, information about access to the health system, and other information about the socioeconomic status of children below the age of five and the mothers (aged between 15 and 49). The DHS data sets also contain information on cluster characteristics, especially on infrastructure. This information is included in the service availability recodes that are available for the South Asian countries Bangladesh (2000) and India (1999) and in Sub-Saharan Africa for Mali (2001), Uganda (1995), and Zimbabwe (1994). In total, our sample contains more than 53.000 children in South Asia and more than 29.000 children in Sub-Saharan Africa.

The underlying theoretical framework for the choice of the dependent and independent variables to study child mortality and undernutrition, i.e. the underlying determinants, closely follows the analytical framework proposed by Molsey and Chen (1984) to study child survival. The idea of this framework is the assumption that social, economic, demographic, and medical determinants, i.e. the proximate determinants, affect the survival probability of the children through a set of biological mechanism. The proximate determinants are grouped at different hierarchial levels, i.e. the individual, household, and community level. In this analysis, the Mosley and Chen (1984) framework is combined with the conceptual framework to study the causes of child undernutrition proposed by the United Nations Childrens' Fund (UNICEF, 1990), which is based on assumptions similar to the Mosley and Chen (1984) framework, and the subsequent extended model of Engle et al. (1999), which implements also the provision of health care capacities of households into the analysis of childrens' welfare.

As dependent variables, we use two dummy variables. For child mortality, the dummy is used whether the child died in the first year of life.[13] To measure child undernutrition, the DHS data sets provide information on several anthropometric outcomes of children, in particular the z-scores for weight for age, weight for

---

[13]To capture the whole birth history of the children, we do not consider child mortality of children below the age of five because this throws out to many observations. We do not explicitly separate between neonatal deaths (child died in the first month) and post-neonatal death (child died between the first month and the first year of life (Adebayo et al., 2004) because this did not change the results.

height, and height for age.[14] In line with the dependent variable for child mortality, as dependent variable for child mortality, we use a dummy variable whether the child is stunted, that is, whether the stunting z-score (height for age) is below -2 standard deviations from the median of the reference population (WHO, 1995, 2006).[15] In addition, we also use the stunting z-scores as the dependent variable to study the determinants of undernutrition.

In the empirical model, we include a set of several individual and household characteristics as well as cluster characteristics that might have an effect on the two outcome variables. For the individual characteristics, besides the household size and the number of children in the household, we include the age and sex of the child in the regression equation. The nutritional status is supposed to worsen non-linearly with increasing age of the child, and with the sex variable we control for sex differentials in mortality and undernutrition in our countries as is often to be found in the empirical literature on child mortality and undernutrition (for example, see Marcoux, 2002; Klasen, 1996). Another major determinant focussing especially on child mortality is the question whether the child was immediately breastfed after birth. Breastfeeding in the first month of life plays an important role for the development of the child because the breastmilk meets most of the childs' nutritional needs and increases the childs' resistance against diseases (Ramalingaswami et al., 1996). To avoid the problem of endogeneity when including breastfeeding and the birth order number of the child in our regression model, i.e. that these variables are affected by the age of the child, we include a dummy whether the child was breastfed immediately after birth and a dummy whether the child is the first born child in the household. In addition, we include also a variable that shows the preceding birth interval, and a variable that indicates whether the vaccination process of the child is completed, which is expected to decrease the mortality risk of the child. To avoid the problem of endogeneity, the dummy whether the vaccination process is completed is defined as follows: the first 2 month after birth are not considered as incomplete if no vaccinations were received, for the age between 3 and 6 months the dummy is one if the child has received at least 3 vaccinations, for the age between 7 and 9 months if the child has received at least 6 vaccinations and between 10 and 12 months if the child has received all 8 vaccinations.

---

[14]The z-score is defined as: $z = \frac{AI_i - MAI}{\sigma}$, where AI_i refers to the individual anthropometric indicator (height for age - stunting, weight for height - underweight, weight for age - wasting), MAI refers to the median of the reference population, and σ refers to the standard deviation of the reference population. For example, the stunting z-scores are the outcomes of the ratio of height over age minus the median of the reference population and the standard deviation of the reference population (see e.g. Klasen, 2003, 2007; Smith and Haddad, 2000).

[15]We also consider the case of extreme stunted children where the z-score is below -3 standard deviations of the height for age reference.

Concerning the mother, the educational level of the mother enters the regression equation. The argument here is twofold. First, more-educated women might be able to better process information and to acquire skills in order to take care of the children, for example in the case of illness, and second, better-educated women are in a better position to earn money. In addition, the nutritional status of the mother is included, which is supposed to strongly affect the nutritional status of the child.[16] In particular, a bad nutritional status is expected to have a severe negative impact especially on the nutritional status of the child. Strong empirical evidence exist that show a high risk of low birth weight and birth height for children whose mother has suffered by a bad nutritional status (see e.g. Rao et al., 2001; Hasin et al., 1996; Smith and Haddad, 2000). As a proxy for the status of women within the household, we include the age of the mother at the time of the survey. To take into account the household structure, we include the household size into the model. As a strong argument can be made that the household size is endogenous, the household size enters based on an instrumental variable approach, where the mean household size in the respective cluster is used as instrument.

As we do not have information on income or expenditure in the DHS, we consider an asset-based approach in defining well-being (Sahn and Stifel, 2001). For this, we use a principal component analysis on several household assets proposed by Filmer and Pritchett (2001) to derive an index that indicates the material status of a household. In particular, as the components for the asset index, we include dummies whether the following assets exist or not: radio, TV, refrigerator, bike, motorized transport, low floor material, toilet, drinking water. Of course, one could include the assets separately into the regression, but the use of an aggregate index has two main reasons: First, it provides an income proxy of the household, which can be used to analyze distributional differences of outcomes in child mortality and undernutrition. Second, as the assets are correlated, their coefficients are likely to provide no significant effects if they are included separately, which would however lead to misleading interpretations of the estimation results. We then introduce another index into the analysis, which includes information on the access to health facilities of the household. Again, this is based on a principal component analysis using dummies whether the mother has received a tetanus vaccination before birth, whether the mother has received prenatal care, and whether the child was born at home without assistance of a doctor or a nurse. We assume that the access to health facilities is a crucial determinant both for child mortality and undernutrition. This index captures both the potential access

---

[16]The recommend method to measure the nutritional status of adults is the body mass index (BMI), which is calculated by $BMI = weight(kg)/height^2(m^2)$. A mother is considered as malnourished if her BMI is less then 18.5

opportunities to the health system as well as real outcomes, which means that the child or the mother have really benefited from the services. To make the coefficients of the asset index and the access to health facility index comparable across regions and countries, the calculation of both indices are based on a global data set, which includes all country samples.

Besides the individual and household characteristics, we include cluster variables.[17] In this context, the multilevel model distinguishes two different kinds of variables, namely contextual variables and global variables. Contextual variables at higher levels are variables that are simply the aggregates of the covariates at the individual level for each cluster. For example, we include the percentage of women with secondary education per cluster and the percentage of children that had recently suffered from fever per cluster. The global variables are part of the service availability recode and are not drawn from information of the individual level. In our case, these global variables provide information about the infrastructure in the cluster. We include the distance to the next health facility, which might be important for the access to heath services, and a public infrastructure index that is based on the availability of general facilities like a bank, a cinema, a post office, primary and secondary schools, a telephone, and public transportation. The weights for the index again are determined by a principal component analysis.

3.3.2   Descriptive Statistics

As can be seen in Table 3.1, the South Asia - Sub-Saharan Africa Enigma of anthropometric failure and mortality reversals is clearly discernable in our five data sets. Relatively higher undernutrition rates in both South Asian countries coincide with relatively lower infant mortality rates than in the three Sub-Saharan African countries. For example, whereas the infant mortality rate in Mali is 1.9 times higher than in India (149 compared to 79), the stunting rate in India is 15 percent higher than in Mali (43.17 compared to 37.61). This result is independent of the measure for undernutrition (i.e. stunting, wasting, underweight or the composite index of (severe) anthropometric failure (CIAF/CISAF) that indicates undernutrition by any of the preceding measures).[18] For example, whereas Bangladesh and Zimbabwe show almost equal mortality rates (80 compared to 75), the rate of severely underweight children is four times higher in Bangladesh than in Zimbabwe (13.12 and 3.26, respectively). This picture is not changed by the use of the new multi-country growth reference standard that was published by the WHO

---

[17]In the case of India, the service availability recode contains information on districts instead of clusters.

[18]In particular, CIAF and CISAF indicate whether a child is (severely) undernourished by either stunting, wasting, or underweight.

in 2006. Prevalence rates using this new reference standard are shown in parentheses. Table 3.1 shows that the anthropometric indicators that are based on the new reference standard lie all above the indicators based on the old reference standard. For example, the stunting rate in Bangladesh increases from 44.12 percent to 50.82 percent. However, this level effect does not change the picture of the Enigma, because the ratios of anthropometric indicators between South Asia and Sub-Saharan Africa do not change very much. For instance, the stunting ratio between India and Mali is 1.16 for the old standard and 1.17 for the new standard. This result suggests that the use of new reference standard instead of the old reference standard is not able to solve the Enigma alone.

Table 3.1: Infant Mortality and Anthropometric Indicators
(percentage)

	Bangladesh 2000	India 1999	Mali 2001	Uganda 1995	Zimbabwe 1994
Infant mortality					
Infant mortality*	80	79	149	99	75
Undernutrition**					
Stunting	44.12	43.17	37.61	35.19	22.24
	(50.82)	(50.75)	(43.06)	(42.37)	(30.09)
Wasting	10.50	14.99	10.97	5.11	5.56
	(13.47)	(20.09)	(13.83)	(7.34)	(7.30)
Underweight	47.32	43.77	34.14	23.38	16.30
	(41.48)	(40.62)	(30.62)	(19.81)	(12.54)
Severe stunting	18.12	21.39	19.01	13.26	6.18
	(24.39)	(30.31)	(24.44)	(19.20)	(10.28)
Severe wasting	1.05	2.84	1.72	0.85	0.86
	(3.36)	(8.49)	(5.48)	(3.02)	(2.99)
Severe underweight	13.12	15.92	11.66	6.12	3.26
	(14.41)	(18.21)	(12.97)	(7.19)	(3.39)
CIAF***	56.63	57.21	47.86	41.21	29.82
	(61.10)	(63.58)	(52.05)	(47.01)	(36.09)
CISAF	22.16	27.33	22.85	15.39	8.05
	(29.64)	(38.37)	(29.42)	(22.37)	(13.26)

Source: Demographic and Health Surveys (DHS); own calculations.
Note: *Child mortality shows the number of dead children per 1000 of children under one year of age who died within the last 12 month. **Children are considered as wasted, stunted, or underweight if the respective z-scores are below -2 standard deviation from the median of the reference category (WHO, 1995). If the z-scores are below -3, children are considered as severely undernourished. The numbers in parentheses refer to the new reference standard for child anthropometric failure that was published by WHO in 2006 (WHO, 2006). ***CIAF and CISAF refer to the composite index of (severe) anthropometric failure that indicates whether a child is (severely) undernourished by either stunting, wasting, or underweight.

Table 3.2 presents summary descriptive statistics of individual, household, and community characteristics four the five countries of our sample. Besides some

Table 3.2: Summary Statistics
for Individual, Household and Community Characteristics

	Bangladesh 2000	India 1999	Mali 2001	Uganda 1995	Zimbabwe 1994
Total number of children in DHS	6.944	46.569	14.328	5.799	2.438
Individual characteristics					
Age (month)	28.79	17.14	28.56	22.63	17.50
Immediate breastfeeding (%)	35.05	25.81	42.40	59.13	53.08
Household characteristics					
Household size	6.79	7.41	7.35	6.59	6.89
Total number children	3.11	2.90	4.67	4.16	3.54
Female headed household (%)	5.36	6.53	8.70	20.28	32.77
Household has					
TV (%)	17.98	38.37	16.07	5.87	12.29
Radio (%)	31.52	41.73	73.06	49.19	43.34
Flush toiled (%)	10.93	25.32	7.19	3.21	22.38
Piped drinking water (%)	6.37	40.04	27.06	12.58	31.27
Mothers' education (years)	3.19	3.90	0.91	4.13	6.38
Mother has no education (%)	45.36	50.14	83.68	26.38	12.92
Mother has primary education (%)	28.96	16.21	11.33	57.76	51.27
Mother has secondary education (%)	21.18	24.45	4.62	15.67	34.58
Age at first birth	17.67	19.35	18.21	18.11	18.96
BMI of mother	19.42	19.83	22.07	21.92	23.00
BMI of mother <18.5 (%)	41.63	34.85	8.33	7.77	5.28
Community characteristics					
Number of vaccinations	5.44	4.65	3.83	5.03	5.82
Birth assistance					
Assistance at birth** (%)	14.31	44.39	22.43	44.16	67.80
Prenatal care (%)	22.51	62.88	20.88	90.46	93.55
Tetanus vaccination (%)	62.37	75.79	31.37	81.25	82.53
Born home w/o assist. (%)	85.24	55.08	60.85	22.77	31.17
Distance to health facility***	47.67****	10.05	7.87	8.69	16.19
Children had fever recently (%)	37.81	30.27	31.08	48.17	37.73

Source: Demographic and Health Surveys (DHS); own calculations.
Notes: *Child was breastfed immediately after birth. **By doctor or nurse. ***Distance to hospital and clinic in kilometers. ****As the distance to the next health facility is not included in the data set for Bangladesh the time in minutes to next health facility is used.

observed similarities in the household and child characteristics, Table 3.2 shows also large differences in the covariates both between South Asia and Sub-Saharan Africa and within these regions between countries. First, looking at regional differences in the individual, household, and community characteristics between South Asia and Sub-Saharan Africa, they provide first insights of possible explanations of the Enigma. For example, Table 3.2 shows that both the share of mothers who breastfed their children immediately after birth and the share of female headed households are considerably higher in Sub-Saharan Africa than in

South Asia. If female headed households are less able to care for their children, than the high share in Sub-Saharan Africa can contribute to the existing relative high rates of child mortality. In addition, Table 3.2 shows also very large region-specific differences in the nutritional status of the mothers, which is much worse in South Asia than in Sub-Saharan Africa. In particular, whereas in Bangladesh 41.63 percent of mothers have a BMI less than 18.5, in Zimbabwe 'only' 5.28 percent are malnourished. This regional disparity is also reflected in the low mean values of the BMI of mothers in South Asia compared to countries in Sub-Saharan Africa. This regional pattern is very interesting since the nutritional status of the mother is expected to have a strong negative impact on the nutritional status of the child, which would then help to explain the Enigma. Various empirical studies exist, which analyze the reasons for the high prevalence of malnourished mothers in South Asia. Primarily, gender differences in the socio-economic status of women are identified as the most important determinants of the low BMI of mothers in Bangladesh, particularly in urban areas (see e.g. Ahmed et al., 1998). In India, women in rural areas are more likely to work full-time in farming activities than men and carry also the burden of the work in the household, which often results in chronic fatigue and undernutrition (see e.g. Barker et al., 2006). If the nutritional status of the the mother increases the risk of child undernutrition, this would then contribute to explain the higher rates of stunting in South Asia compared to Sub-Saharan Africa and contributes to explain the Enigma.

Second, country specific differences between covariates provide also interesting information regarding the explanation of the Enigma. For example, although an overall low level of mothers' education is observed for all five countries, in Mali, which was found to be country with highest mortality rates in our sample, the mean years of education of mothers is less than 1 year, compared to 6.38 years in Zimbabwe, where mortality rates and rates of child undernutrition were found to be rather low. Hence, given that Bangladesh, India, and Zimbabwe show relatively high levels of education and low levels of child mortality, this suggests that the educational attainment might be an important determinant for the survival probabilities of children. However, as argued in the previous section, the educational level of mothers is also expected to have an important impact on the nutritional status of the child, but Bangladesh and India show the highest rates of undernutrition. Other glaring differences between countries are found for some community characteristics, particular the access to health infrastructure. Bangladesh has the lowest rates of assistance at birth (14.31) and of prenatal care (22.51), Zimbabwe has the best access to birth assistance in the sample, with 67.8 percent of mothers who have received assistance at birth and even 93.55 percent who received prenatal care. Looking at the difference in stunting and child mortality, this result suggests a strong influence of access to health care on both outcomes of childrens' welfare.

As mentioned before, the lack of income data necessitates the use of a wealth index as a proxy for incomes or consumption. To avoid using arbitrary weights, we use a principal component analysis, which implies that the weights are equivalent to a measure of the degree of correlation between each factor and a hidden component (in our case wealth). First, the results of the principal component analysis, which are presented in Table A.1 in Appendix A, show that all weights for the factors have the assumed sign, giving positive values to durable goods like TV and radio and negative values to the lack of a toilet facility or the use of surface drinking water. Second, also when we look at the weights of our health facility index, it can be seen that the principal component analysis determines weights with the 'right' signs, which is shown in Table A.1 in Appendix A. Positive weights are generated, therefore, for the dummies for a tetanus vaccination of the mother before birth, and for prenatal care. A negative value is generated for the dummy whether a child was born at home without the assistance of a doctor or a nurse.

In addition, the results of the principal component analysis show that both factors, wealth and access to health facilities are strongly correlated with child mortality and undernutrition. First, Table 3.3 reflects the differences in the levels of child mortality and undernutrition between the two regions and between countries, and confirms the Enigma. Second, Table 3.3 show that both phenomena are a lot more prevalent in the lower quintiles of both indices meaning that the poor population is much more affected by child mortality and undernutrition than the non-poor population. As the distribution of both phenomena over the indices shows a similar pattern across regions and countries, a particularly strong connection is observable between access to health facilities and child mortality indicating that the development of the health care system is a very strong determinant for probability of the child to survive. Here, for example, the ratio of the first to the fifth quintile in Bangladesh is 9.70, and India, Uganda, and Mali even show no child mortality for their respective fifth quintile.

3.3.3   Regression Results

This section presents the regression results and discusses possible explanations of the South Asia - Sub-Saharan Africa Enigma that were asked in Section 3.1.2. First, it starts with comparing the multilevel approach to standard regression models when analyzing child mortality and undernutrition. Second, to shed more light on the South Asia - Sub-Saharan Africa Enigma, this section discusses the differences in the determinants of child mortality and undernutrition to explain the relationship between both phenomena. In particular, the results provide us with information about socio-economic characteristics that determine child mortality and undernutrition in a similar way and characteristics that determine both phenomena in different ways, which helps to explain the Enigma. Third, regional dif-

Table 3.3: Mortality and Stunting by Asset and Access to Health Facility Index (percentage)

	Quintile 1	Quintile 2	Quintile 3	Quintile 4	Quintile 5	Ratio 1/5
			Asset index			
Infant mortality						
Bangladesh 2000	9.26	8.21	8.03	8.12	6.33	1.46
India 1999	10.32	8.43	7.64	7.20	5.69	1.81
Mali 2001	16.54	16.41	15.12	14.41	11.92	1.39
Uganda 1995	11.27	11.16	9.86	9.21	8.46	1.33
Zimbabwe 1994	8.98	7.74	6.50	6.50	8.05	1.12
Stunting						
Bangladesh 2000	54.49	49.46	43.01	32.81	16.74	3.26
India 1999	53.11	47.48	44.21	41.16	33.15	1.60
Mali 2001	46.84	40.70	40.62	37.20	23.83	1.97
Uganda 1995	41.57	37.98	31.10	21.77	16.48	2.52
Zimbabwe 1994	22.13	28.12	25.40	20.90	12.43	1.78
			Access to health facilities index			
Infant mortality						
Bangladesh 2000	21.72	7.25	7.51	0.81	2.24	9.70
India 1999	15.16	10.80	8.97	3.80	0	n.c.
Mali 2001	21.59	17.29	16.07	11.15	8.08	2.67
Uganda 1995	19.98	16.99	11.12	1.07	0	n.c.
Zimbabwe 1994	23.84	6.52	6.50	0	0	n.c.
Stunting						
Bangladesh 2000	56.62	45.90	46.73	31.90	17.51	3.23
India 1999	56.21	54.31	44.64	37.66	31.89	1.76
Mali 2001	43.06	39.85	35.21	21.27	17.16	2.51
Uganda 1995	36.96	39.54	36.32	34.36	33.94	1.09
Zimbabwe 1994	27.71	26.60	21.61	22.52	21.25	1.30

Source: Demographic and Health Surveys (DHS); own calculations.
Notes: Infant mortality shows the percentage of children under 1 year of age who died within the last 12 months compared to all children under one year of age living in the respective quintile. The stunting rate shows the percentage of stunted children in the respective quintile compared to all children under 5 years of age. A child is considered as stunted if the height over age z-score is below -2 standard deviations from the reference category. The asset index is calculated based on a principal component analysis. As variables to calculate the asset index, dummies are included whether the following assets exist or not in a household: radio, TV, refrigerator, bike, motorized transport, low floor material, toilet, drinking water. Quintile 1 corresponds to the poorest and quintile 5 to the richest population sub-group.

ferences between South Asia and Sub-Saharan Africa and also country-specific differences in the regression results are discussed concerning possible explanations of the Enigma.

As mentioned before, we use a multilevel model approach to examine the influence of individual, household, and community socio-economic characteristics on child mortality (Table 3.4) and child undernutrition (Tables 3.5 and 3.6). The use of a multilevel approach instead of standard regression models insures that we avoid misleading significance effects due to violations of the assumption of independent errors with a constant variance. This effect is confirmed in our regression results in which the multilevel regressions display lower levels of significance compared to the OLS regression and the logit regression with the same model specification, which are presented in Tables A.2-A.6 in Appendix A. The standard errors for the multilevel regression are higher than the standard errors for the logit and OLS regressions for mortality and for undernutrition both using a dummy whether the child is stunted and also using the stunting z-scores as dependent variable. Especially, in the case of community characteristics, a strong reduction in significance levels is observable, whereas for the individual and household characteristics the differences in significance of the coefficients are rather low. This means that the multilevel approach allows a more reliable analysis of the determinants of our household survey data through explicitly incorporating the hierarchical data structure of the data and community information.

Turning to the estimation results and possible explanations of the South Asia - Sub-Saharan Africa Enigma, Tables 3.4-3.6 show the regression results for infant mortality and stunting both for the old and the new reference standard. As expected, the age of the mother has a significant non-linear negative influence on child mortality in all cases, meaning that the number of child deaths decreases non-linearly with age, which reflects the increasing experience of mothers to take care of their children when they got older compared to very young mothers. At the same time, the age of the child influences undernutrition positively in a well known non-linear way in all countries as is also shown in Figure 3.1, which presents the stunting z-score by age for the respective country and reference standard.[19] Figure 3.1 shows that the stunting z-scores strongly decrease within the first two years of live and then remain constant or starts to raise slowly. This pattern of decreasing z-scores in early childhood can be explained by the critical phase for the child when the mother replaces breast milk to complementary food or liquids. If the mother stops breastfeeding, the child is exposed to malnutrition and diseases, particularly if the complementary food is nutritionally inadequate or not hygienic (see e.g. UNICEF, 1998; Klasen, 2007). Again, as described in Section 3.3.2, Figure 3.1 demonstrates the differences in the levels of the z-scores between the old and the new reference standard to calculate the z-scores.

Concerning the relationship between child mortality and undernutrition and their respective determinants, Tables 3.4 through 3.6 show that mortality and undernutrition have both very similar determinants across countries and also determinants that affect both phenomena in different way. The results are confirmed when using the stunting z-scores as dependent variable. Very similar effects across countries are found when looking at individual characteristics like immediate

---

[19]For India and Zimbabwe, the DHS provide information on anthropometric indicators for children only until the age of 3 years.

breastfeeding. As expected, a positive breastfeeding practice like the immediate initiation of breastfeeding after birth has a negative and, in most cases, a significant effect on mortality. This complies with the general observation of the importance of the colostrum, which contains a large number of antibodies and basically works as a first immunization or vaccination. Furthermore, a strong and significant decreasing effect on the mortality risk is found if the vaccination process of the child is complete. In addition, also the preceding birth interval has a positive effect the survival probability and the nutritional status of the child. Analogous to this findings, we also find a consistent pattern of the effect of the household structure, measured by the household size, which enters based on a instrumental variable approach. The household size increases both the mortality risk and the risk of undernutrition.

Tables 3.4, 3.5, and 3.6 also show determinants that affect mortality and undernutrition in different directions and at different significance levels. For example, being the first born significantly decreases the risk of being malnourished in all countries except of Zimbabwe. In contrast, a positive but insignificant effect was found for the risk of dying within the first year of life. Interesting to note is that we find no clear gender bias in a way that girls have higher mortality risks than boys. Being female even has a significant negative effect on the mortality risk in Mali. This might be due to the higher susceptibility of boys to diseases in early years, which also results in a worse nutritional status of boys. Particularly, when using the new reference standard, we find significantly lower undernutrition rates for girls. In addition, being a girl significantly increases the risk of being stunted in South Asia, whereas it decreases the risk of undernutrition in Sub-Saharan Africa.

Differences in the determinants are not only found in different directions of the coefficients but also in different magnitudes of the impacts and different significance levels. For example, whereas the asset index strongly influences the nutritional status of children in all five countries, no such overall significant effect was found for the mortality risk. Here, only India shows a significant reducing effect of the asset index on mortality. The effect of the asset index on undernutrition reflects that material welfare strongly increases the capacities to care for children, resulting in higher investments in children and higher outcomes of their status of well-being, but also that it seems to be more important for the nutritional status of the child rather for the probability of the child to survive. In addition, whereas a strong impact on the child mortality risk was found if the vaccination process of the child is complete, no such clear effect is found for undernutrition. Another difference concerning the determinants of child mortality and undernutrition is found for the nutritional status of the mother, measured by the BMI. As already discussed in Section 3.3.2, the nutritional status of the mother has a very strong effect on the nutritional status of the child. What is interesting to note here is that when looking at the results of undernutrition based on the new reference standard,

Table A.8 shows that the BMI of the mother affects the childs' nutritional status non-linearity way in Bangladesh, which is reflected in the BMI squared, in the sense that the positive effect decreases with high values of BMI (see also Kandala et al., 2001). This reflects the possibility that the high BMI is simply due to the intake of many calories that are, however, nutritionally inadequate. In contrast, the nutritional status of the mother seems to play no significant role for the probability of the child to survive.

In addition, also the mothers' educational attainment affects both phenomena in different ways. We found a clear negative and significant effect if the mother has achieved secondary schooling level on undernutrition both at the individual level and also at the community level, measured as the percent of secondary education in the cluster. In contrast, and quite surprisingly, the educational attainment of the mothers exhibits a much lower influence on child mortality than originally expected. One explanation might be that the mothers' education level seems to have no clear direct significant influence on child mortality and only influences it indirectly via other determinants like better feeding practices and lower fertility, instead. Thus, as was also found for the asset index and the nutritional status of mother, the mothers' educational attainment is more important for undernutrition than for mortality.

When also taking into account regional and country-specific differences between the determinants of mortality and undernutrition, Tables 3.4-3.6 provide interesting results that also can help to explain the Enigma. On the one hand, the largest and most significant effect on mortality is exerted by the access to health facilities, which is measured by our health facility index and which strongly decreases the mortality risk of children. This index includes information on whether the mother received prenatal care as well as a tetanus injection before birth, whether the child was born at home without the assistance of a doctor or a nurse and on the mean number of vaccinations per child in a household. On the other hand, the health index has no such clear effect on child undernutrition. Whereas the health index strongly decreases the risk of being malnourished in South Asia, Zimbabwe is the only country in Sub-Saharan Africa where the index shows a significant negative effect. First, this results suggest that the access to health facilities is more important for mortality than for undernutrition and, second that in South Asia, the access to health facilities is also more important to reduce undernutrition than in Sub-Saharan Africa.[20] Another regional difference is found for the preceding birth interval in the case of infant mortality. Here, we found a significant reducing effect only for the Sub-Saharan African countries, whereas the effect is smaller and not significant in South Asia. Therefore, an overall short time period between

---

[20]However, looking at the regression results of the logit regression model, Table A.3 shows also an overall high and significant effect of the health index on undernutrition.

two births would contribute to the relatively higher mortality rates in Sub-Saharan Africa compared to South Asia.

Looking at the effects of the community characteristics, except for the percentage of secondary education per cluster, we find only very small effects on child mortality and undernutrition for other variables at the community level when using the multilevel approach. This is the case despite the variation of the intercept of the community level σ_u^2 being significant and, therefore, showing that information of this level plays a role in explaining child mortality.[21] However, especially the results of the higher level covariates show large country-specific differences. For example, only for Uganda and Zimbabwe, we find a significant mortality increasing effect of the public infrastructure index and no significant reducing effect on undernutrition at all. The percentage of children with fever in a cluster significantly increases the mortality risk only in Bangladesh and Uganda, but it has a clear negative effect on undernutrition in India, Mali, and Uganda. These examples of differences in the determinants and their significance levels between countries reflect that the Enigma cannot only be solved by identifying region-specific determinants of child molality and undernutrition but that also country-specific variations play an important role.

After concentrating on the country-specific regression results and the differences and similarities of infant mortality and undernutrition, we now turn again directly to differences and similarities between the two regions of South Asia and Sub-Saharan Africa. Table 3.7 shows the additional regressions that were implemented using a combined data set of all children in the five countries, which confirm the results of the country regressions. In addition to the covariates of the country-specific regression models, Table 3.7 includes also a region dummy for Sub-Saharan Africa that captures the unexplained part of the Enigma and also some interactions between Sub-Saharan Africa and individual and community characteristics. The region dummy for Sub-Saharan Africa in Table 3.7 shows that the Enigma still remains and underlines that significant differences between the two regions still exist, even when we control for the large set of explanatory variables. Whereas the dummy variable for Sub-Saharan Africa has a strong significant positive effect on mortality, it has a strong negative effect on undernutrition. In particular, the first row in Table 3.7 shows that mortality is significantly larger in Sub-Saharan Africa than in South Asia and the second and third row show that it is the other way round when we look at stunting, both for the old and the new reference standard. Besides the significant region dummy, the inclusion of region interaction effects shows that the coefficients for almost all variables differ significantly between regions. For example, the effect of the interaction of

---

[21]Again, higher significance for the variables at the community level are found for the logit and OLS regression (see Tables A.2-A.6 in Appendix C).

female headed households and Sub-Saharan Africa shows a strong negative impact on mortality. The same holds for the effect of immediate breastfeeding and for the effect of a complete vaccination process on child mortality. In addition, also the effect of the access to health facility on child mortality and the asset index on undernutrition are significantly higher in Sub-Saharan Africa than in South Asia. In contrast, the effect of the percentage of children with fever on undernutrition is lower in Sub-Saharan Africa than in South Asia. What is also interesting to note is that if the nutritional status of mother is interacted with the Sub-Saharan Africa dummy, this shows no clear significant decreasing effect, whereas it does for South Asia.

To summarize the estimation results, we have found that, first, the multilevel approach allows to correct for too high significance levels compared to standard regression models. Second, the estimation results provide new insights for solving the South Asia - Sub-Saharan Africa Enigma. Concerning the relationship between mortality and undernutrition, we have identified determinants that affect both phenomena in a similar way like breastfeeding. However, we have also found differences in the determinants between child mortality and undernutrition. In particular, the material welfare, the nutritional status of the mother, and her educational attainment are relatively more important to reduce undernutrition risk, whereas a complete vaccination process and the access to health facility are relatively more important to reduce the mortality risk of children. Thus, although similar determinants of both phenomena are identified, both phenomena are not perfectly correlated, which would then also allow to explain some of the differences in the outcomes in the two regions. In particular, the low levels of the mothers' BMI in South Asia can partly explain the high levels of child undernutrition in Bangladesh and India. Moreover, we have also found large regional and country-specifics differences in the determinants of mortality and undernutrition concerning their magnitude and significance levels, which can also help to explain the Enigma. For example, the access to health facilities is relatively more important in Sub-Saharan Africa. This seems to be very important to explain the relatively high mortality rates in this region, since countries in Sub-Saharan Africa face higher risks of infectious diseases induced by the tropical climate like Malaria and also face much higher risks of HIV infections, which is supposed to be a strong determinant of mortality and which cannot be observed by our data set. In addition, we also found that country-specific factors are important that show no regional trend and that countries in Sub-Saharan Africa differ among each other as well as countries in South Asia. However, even if we have identified some factors that can help to explain part of the Enigma, the global regression has shown that still much behind the Enigma persists, which can not be solved by our regression results.

Figure 3.1: Mean Stunting Z-Scores By Age

(a)
(old reference standard)

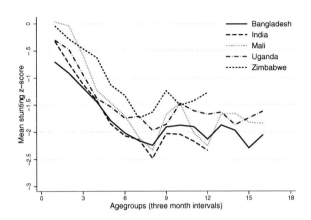

(b)
(new reference standard)

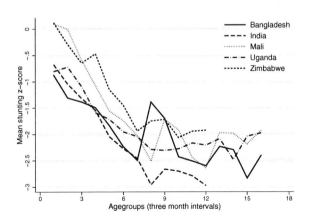

Source: Demographic and Health Surveys (DHS); own calculations.

3.3.4   Simulations

To shed more light on the South Asia - Sub-Saharan Africa Enigma, in this section, we take explicitly into account the regional and country-specific differences between the outcomes of individual, household, and community characteristics and their respective effects on mortality and undernutrition. We compare the effects of covariates on undernutrition and child mortality by simulating the effects for cases, in where one country would have the outcome and the distribution of covariates of another country. In particular, we create rank preserving transformations of selected covariates between countries. This means, for example that we assign the value of the best educated mother in Uganda to the best educated mother in India. Thus, we ask what would be the outcome of child mortality or undernutrition if the mothers in India had the same level and distribution of education as mothers in Uganda.

We simulate the effects on child mortality and undernutrition based on this rank preserving transformation for a large set of several covariates and countries in South Asia and Sub-Saharan Africa. For example, based on the result that the nutritional status of mothers has a greater impact on child undernutrition in South Asia, we assign the outcome and the distribution of the BMI of mothers from Mali to mothers in India and Bangladesh and estimate the difference in the effect on undernutrition. However, we found an overall small effect. If mothers in India and Bangladesh had the nutritional status of mothers from Mali, this would change the rate of undernutrition of 0.2 percent and 0.3 percent, respectively. In addition, since also the educational attainment of mothers has a greater effect on undernutrition in South Asia, we assign the education of the mothers from Uganda to the mothers in Bangladesh and India. But also here, the effect is only very small.

Furthermore, based on the result that the access to health facilities has a larger impact on child mortality in Sub-Saharan Africa, we assign the values and the distribution of the access to health facilities index from India to Mali. Here, we found that mortality would decrease in Mali by 2 percent if Mali had the access to health facilities as India. However, for the case, where we assign the asset index of Bangladesh to Uganda and Zimbabwe, we only find a very small effect on mortality in both countries.

Concerning the explanations of the South Asia - Sub-Saharan Africa Enigma, non of these simulations had the potential to fully explain it. But using these simulations, we were able to test the economic significance of the different explanatory variables, meaning that we were able to see what effects certain improvements in the different determinants have on both phenomena. One clear result was that changes in the explanatory variables would result in very different changes in the two forms of deprivation. Again, the strongest influence on child mortality is exerted by the access to health facilities. Although the influence on stunting was also very significant, the magnitude was by far not as large. At the same time, we confirmed the preceding results that increases in material wealth will result in significant reductions of undernutrition and mortality. Even stronger improvements in the incidence of undernutrition could be generated by increases in the level of education of mothers, which has only a limited positive effect on changes in mortality rates by it own.

3.4 Conclusion

In this paper, we analyzed the regional puzzle of child mortality and undernutrition between South Asia and Sub-Sahara Africa. We investigated the effects of individual, household and community socio-economic characteristics on child mortality and undernutrition using a multilevel approach for a set of five developing countries in South Asia and Sub-Saharan Africa. We find strong evidence supporting the existence of the South Asia Sub-Saharan Africa Enigma using micro-data.

The results show large differences in the determinants and their significance levels between mortality and undernutrition, across the two regions, and also between countries. While finding very similar patterns across countries indicating a close relationship between child mortality and undernutrition, we also find that the determinants of mortality and undernutrition differ significantly from each other, which helps to explain the Enigma. And although very similar patterns in the determinants of each phenomenon are discernable, there are large differences in the magnitude of the coefficients. Accounting for the high rates of child mortality in Sub-Saharan Africa, strong evidence is found that the access to health infrastructure is more important for mortality than for undernutrition and the impact is of greater magnitude in Sub-Saharan Africa than in South Asia, whereas the individual and household characteristics like wealth and educational attainment and nutritional characteristics of mothers play a larger role for anthropometric shortfalls. Especially, the nutritional status of mothers has a greater effect in South Asia accounting partly for the high rates of undernutrition, since the overall nutritional status of the mother is even worse in South Asia than in Sub-Saharan Africa. As our study has also shown, there are determinants at the community level that have a significant influence on mortality as well as on undernutrition like the percentage of children with fever or public infrastructure. Besides, regressions using a combined data set of all five countries show that there are still significant unexplained differences between the two regions although taking account of a large set of covariates. Therefore, our results are only partly be able to solve the Enigma.

One hypothetical explanation for the regional differences remains the quality of the data. There might be biases and errors especially in the African data sets.

However, these biases cannot account for the differences in the determinants of both phenomena, since the same data sets and explanatory variables are used for the explanation of child mortality and undernutrition in all countries.

Explaining the high rates of child mortality in Sub-Saharan Africa, clearly unobserved socio-economic characteristics play an important role. For example Klasen (2003) emphasizes the importance of the mortality decreasing effect of lower fertility. Another possible explanation for the Enigma might lie in the different prevalence of diseases like HIV/AIDS and Malaria, which heavily affects countries in Sub-Saharan Africa. Therefore, given the data constraints on infectious diseases and their consequences at the individual level, further studies should try to estimate the impact of HIV/AIDS and other diseases on mortality rates. Future research should also try to capture differences in the quality of health facilities and in the composition of nourishments.

Accounting for the high rates of undernutrition in South Asia, one possible explanation might still be how undernutrition is measured. Klasen (2007) suggests that measurement issues play a significant role for the high rates of undernutrition in South Asia. He identifies both the arbitrary cut-off of a z-score of -2 and the reference standard by the WHO (old and new) to calculate the z-scores as two important issues that might lead to an overestimation of undernutrition in South Asia. In particular, he emphasizes that already small genetic differences in the growth potential of children in South Asia considerably overestimate undernutrition in South Asia. Therefore, a closer investigation of the role of the genetic differences as a possible explanation for the high rates of undernutrition in South Asia is of high priority. Another reason for the high rates of undernutrition in South Asia could also be the effects of past undernutrition of the mothers during their childhood, which might has an impact on the status of their children, even if they grow up an a healthy and wealthy environment (Klasen, 2007).

To investigate further explanations of the Enigma, high research priority should also be given on other factors like interactions and non-linearities between risk factors and that they might effect child mortality and undernutrition in a rather multiplicative than additive way (see e.g. Pelletier, 1994).

Finally, one part of the explanation of the South Asia Sub-Saharan Africa Enigma could be the insight that child mortality and undernutrition are not as closely correlated as generally assumed. Our study finds considerable evidence for large differences in the determinants of both phenomena. These differences make it highly unlikely that child mortality and undernutrition are as closely correlated as found by the studies of Pelletier et al. (1995, 2002) and cited by numerous other publications. And in order to achieve both Millennium Development Goals concerning child mortality and undernutrition it is, therefore, important that both phenomena are taken into account as separate goals, which are to be achieved by different policy measures.

Table 3.4: Regression Results of Infant Mortality
(Multilevel Regression)

	Bangladesh 2000	India 1999	Mali 2001	Uganda 1995	Zimbabwe 1994
Constant	-3.188**	-2.591**	-2.109**	-2.234**	-2.790**
	(0.111)	(0.043)	(0.061)	(0.118)	(0.222)
Age (mother)	-0.116**	-0.224**	-0.152**	-0.094	-0.182
	(0.062)	(0.031)	(0.034)	(0.067)	(0.157)
Age^2 (mother)	0.170*	0.352**	0.241**	0.133*	0.353
	(0.106)	(0.054)	(0.053)	(0.111)	(0.260)
Sex of child (1=female)	-0.158	0.055	-0.112*	-0.070	-0.410*
	(0.106)	(0.047)	(0.061)	(0.110)	(0.231)
Immediate breastfeeding (=1)	-0.429**	-0.491**	-0.179**	-0.061	-0.501*
	(0.125)	(0.068)	(0.064)	(0.115)	(0.231)
Complete vaccination (=1)	-2.458**	-2.531**	-2.008**	-2.003**	-3.683**
	(0.227)	(0.070)	(0.130)	(0.199)	(0.393)
First born (=1)	0.295	-0.057	-0.095	0.153	0.299
	(0.187)	(0.084)	(0.116)	(0.200)	(0.403)
Preceding birth interval	-0.005	-0.006	-0.015**	-0.009*	0.013*
	(0.003)	(0.002)	(0.002)	(0.005)	(0.005)
Household size (IV)	0.200**	0.105**	0.016**	0.067	0.096
	(0.053)	(0.024)	(0.005)	(0.049)	(0.088)
Female headed household (=1)	0.055	0.100	-0.079	-0.076	-0.012
	(0.258)	(0.100)	(0.111)	(0.147)	(0.251)
Asset index	-0.167	-0.098**	-0.053	-0.145	-0.015
	(0.114)	(0.024)	(0.046)	(0.111)	(0.147)
BMI of mother	-0.042*	0.051	0.026*	-0.045	0.008
	(0.025)	(0.010)	(0.012)	(0.023)	(0.040)
BMI^2/100 of mother	0.484	0.040	-0.281*	0.243	-0.056
	(0.280)	(0.122)	(0.159)	(0.318)	(0.360)
Mother has sec. education (=1)	-0.174	-0.084	-0.313	-0.523**	0.057
	(0.159)	(0.064)	(0.228)	(0.207)	(0.003)
Health facility index	-0.647**	-0.326**	-0.400**	-0.287**	-0.186**
	(0.090)	(0.030)	(0.048)	(0.086)	(0.179)
Community characteristics					
Distance to health facility***	-0.003	0.001	0.002	0.009	0.003
	(0.002)	(0.004)	(0.003)	(0.005)	(0.007)
Secondary education (%)	-0.661	-0.591*	-0.394	0.173	-0.647
	(0.458)	(0.301)	(0.528)	(0.472)	(0.658)
Children had fever (%)	0.775*	-0.330	0.124	0.542*	0.545
	(0.370)	(0.357)	(0.220)	(0.301)	(0.573)
Public infrastruct. index	0.046	-0.002	0.012	0.167*	0.317*
	(0.070)	(0.036)	(0.046)	(0.079)	(0.149)
σ_u^2	0.169	0.255	0.172	0.274	0.698
	(0.086)	(0.042)	(0.041)	(0.108)	(0.375)
R^2	0.099	0.128	0.068	0.068	0.159
Obs. (level 1)	5381	28539	9852	4232	1.568
Obs. (level 2)	339	426	371	357	229

Source: Demographic and Health Surveys (DHS); own calculations.
Notes: *P-value<0.1. **P-value<0.01. For details about the variables, see Section 3.3.1. σ_u^2 refers to the variance of the residual errors of the intercepts at the household level (level 2). ***In the case of Bangladesh distance is measured in time (hours). The household size enters via an instrumental variable into the model. As instrument the mean household size per cluster is used.

Table 3.5: Regression Results of Stunting (Old Reference Standard) (Multilevel Regression)

	Bangladesh 2000	India 1999	Mali 2001	Uganda 1995	Zimbabwe 1994
Constant	-0.601**	-0.326**	-0.644**	-0.776**	-1.459**
	(0.050)	(0.030)	(0.049)	(0.075)	(0.102)
Age (mother)	0.108**	0.247**	0.156**	0.169**	0.305**
	(0.008)	(0.006)	(0.006)	(0.012)	(0.031)
Age^2 (mother)	-0.001**	-0.005**	-0.002**	-0.003**	-0.006**
	(0.000)	(0.000)	(0.000)	(0.000)	(0.001)
Sex of child (1=female)	0.027	0.008	-0.071	-0.241**	-0.049
	(0.061)	(0.025)	(0.049)	(0.069)	(0.115)
Immediate breastfeeding (=1)	-0.131*	-0.010*	-0.120*	-0.052	-0.072
	(0.065)	(0.031)	(0.052)	(0.071)	(0.118)
Complete vaccination (=1)	-0.051	-0.091	-0.111	-0.568	-0.189
	(0.139)	(0.434)	(0.104)	(0.134)	(0.297)
First born (=1)	-0.241*	-0.291**	-0.335**	-0.213*	-0.254
	(0.100)	(0.041)	(0.088)	(0.118)	(0.196)
Preceding birth interval	-0.008**	-0.005**	-0.010**	-0.007**	-0.004
	(0.002)	(0.001)	(0.002)	(0.002)	(0.003)
Household size (IV)	0.034	0.058**	-0.003	-0.047*	0.055
	(0.029)	(0.016)	(0.005)	(0.027)	(0.039)
Female headed household (=1)	-0.161	-0.140**	-0.049	0.057	-0.126
	(0.137)	(0.052)	(0.089)	(0.089)	(0.126)
Asset index	-0.430**	-0.178**	-0.090*	-0.203**	-0.127*
	(0.064)	(0.013)	(0.039)	(0.069)	(0.070)
BMI of mother	-0.090**	-0.065**	-0.075**	-0.073**	-0.060**
	(0.015)	(0.005)	(0.010)	(0.015)	(0.020)
BMI^2/100 of mother	0.309	-0.084*	-0.130	-0.092	0.294
	(0.217)	(0.082)	(0.145)	(0.258)	(0.253)
Mother has sec. education (=1)	-0.354**	-0.251**	-0.561**	-0.291*	-0.346*
	(0.086)	(0.031)	(0.163)	(0.116)	(0.156)
Health facility index	-0.246**	-0.243**	-0.023	-0.061	-0.248**
	(0.047)	(0.017)	(0.036)	(0.059)	(0.086)
Community characteristics					
Distance to health facility***	0.001	-0.004	0.005*	0.006*	0.001
	(0.001)	(0.003)	(0.003)	(0.003)	(0.003)
Secondary education (%)	-0.162	-1.520**	-2.403**	-1.280**	-0.290
	(0.260)	(0.203)	(0.484)	(0.297)	(0.345)
Children had fever (%)	0.215	-0.582*	0.160*	-0.421*	-0.206
	(0.218)	(0.268)	(0.227)	(0.186)	(0.288)
Public infrastruct. index	0.054	-0.021	-0.094	-0.074	-0.025
	(0.042)	(0.024)	(0.046)	(0.054)	(0.081)
σ_u^2	0.097	0.252	0.326	0.134	0.082
	(0.033)	(0.025)	(0.045)	(0.042)	(0.080)
R^2	0.109	0.140	0.118	0.106	0.121
Obs. (level 1)	5284	34797	9258	4518	2057
Obs. (level 2)	339	424	368	354	227

Source: Demographic and Health Surveys (DHS); own calculations.
Notes: *P-value<0.1. **P-value<0.01. For details about the variables, see Section 3.3.1. σ_u^2 refers to the variance of the residual errors of the intercepts at the household level (level 2). ***In the case of Bangladesh distance is measured in time (hours). The household size enters via an instrumental variable into the model. As instrument the mean household size per cluster is used.

Table 3.6: Regression Results of Stunting (New Reference Standard)
(Multilevel Regression)

	Bangladesh 2000	India 1999	Mali 2001	Uganda 1995	Zimbabwe 1994
Constant	-0.243**	0.089**	-0.340**	-0.356**	-0.925**
	(0.046)	(0.030)	(0.046)	(0.069)	(0.091)
Age (child)	0.107**	0.152**	0.135**	0.127**	0.171**
	(0.007)	(0.005)	(0.005)	(0.010)	(0.023)
Age^2 (child)	-0.001**	-0.002**	-0.002**	-0.002**	-0.003**
	(0.000)	(0.000)	(0.000)	(0.000)	(0.001)
Sex of child (1=female)	-0.060	-0.132**	-0.162**	-0.344**	-0.209
	(0.059)	(0.023)	(0.046)	(0.065)	(0.105)
Immediate breastfeeding (=1)	-0.130*	-0.039*	-0.132*	-0.093*	-0.011*
	(0.063)	(0.029)	(0.049)	(0.049)	(0.107)
Complete vaccination (=1)	0.090	0.047	0.204	-0.012	0.177
	(0.130)	(0.038)	(0.092)	(0.198)	(0.244)
First born (=1)	-0.173*	-0.222**	-0.204*	-0.187*	-0.309*
	(0.096)	(0.038)	(0.082)	(0.111)	(0.175)
Preceding birth interval	-0.007**	-0.004**	-0.008**	-0.008**	-0.005
	(0.001)	(0.001)	(0.001)	(0.002)	(0.003)
Household size (IV)	0.012	0.044**	-0.008	-0.043*	0.022
	(0.029)	(0.016)	(0.005)	(0.026)	(0.038)
Female headed household (=1)	-0.112	-0.084	-0.127*	-0.066	-0.126
	(0.132)	(0.048)	(0.084)	(0.084)	(0.114)
Asset index	-0.387**	-0.160**	-0.109**	-0.202**	-0.157**
	(0.061)	(0.012)	(0.036)	(0.065)	(0.068)
BMI of mother	-0.072**	-0.056**	-0.059**	-0.064**	-0.049**
	(0.014)	(0.005)	(0.009)	(0.014)	(0.018)
BMI^2/100 of mother	0.362*	0.000	-0.126	-0.404*	0.157
	(0.155)	(0.001)	(0.244)	(0.244)	(0.216)
Mother has sec. education (=1)	-0.290**	-0.223**	-0.466**	-0.175	-0.260*
	(0.081)	(0.029)	(0.143)	(0.107)	(0.138)
Health facility index	-0.219**	-0.222**	-0.040	-0.085	-0.184*
	(0.046)	(0.016)	(0.034)	(0.055)	(0.080)
Community characteristics					
Distance to health facility***	0.001	-0.006*	0.004	0.010**	0.002
	(0.001)	(0.003)	(0.003)	(0.003)	(0.003)
Secondary education (%)	-0.253	-1.278**	-1.740**	-1.042**	-0.271
	(0.258)	(0.205)	(0.437)	(0.277)	(0.325)
Children with fever (%)	0.276	-0.586*	0.194	-0.470**	-0.124
	(0.217)	(0.273)	(0.218)	(0.178)	(0.276)
Public infrastruct. index	-0.005	-0.020	-0.060	-0.121*	-0.042
	(0.041)	(0.024)	(0.043)	(0.051)	(0.078)
σ_u^2	0.113	0.284	0.312	0.137	0.167
	(0.034)	(0.027)	(0.042)	(0.040)	(0.079)
R^2	0.100	0.114	0.100	0.094	0.097
Obs. (level 1)	5503	37880	9750	4771	2114
Obs. (level 2)	339	424	368	355	227

Source: Demographic and Health Surveys (DHS); own calculations.
Notes: *P-value<0.1. **P-value<0.01. For details about the variables, see Section 3.3.1. σ_u^2 refers to the variance of the residual errors of the intercepts at the household level (level 2). ***In the case of Bangladesh distance is measured in time (hours). The household size enters via an instrumental variable into the model. As instrument the mean household size per cluster is used.

Table 3.7: Global Regression of Infant Mortality and Stunting
(Multilevel Regression)

	Infant mortality		Stunting (old ref. standard)		Stunting (new ref. standard)	
Constant	-2.694**	(0.054)	-0.445**	(0.029)	-0.036**	(0.028)
Age	-0.158**	(0.019)	0.147**	(0.003)	0.126**	(0.002)
Age^2	0.245**	(0.031)	-0.002**	(0.000)	-0.002**	(0.000)
Sex of child (1=female)	-0.033	(0.033)	-0.023	(0.019)	-0.141**	(0.018)
Immediate breastfeeding (=1)	-0.472**	(0.057)	-0.089**	(0.025)	-0.104**	(0.024)
Complete vaccination (=1)	-2.438**	(0.063)	-0.102**	(0.038)	-0.020	(0.035)
First born (=1)	0.025	(0.072)	-0.297**	(0.036)	-0.235**	(0.033)
Preceding birth interval	-0.005**	(0.001)	-0.005**	(0.001)	-0.004**	(0.001)
Household size (IV)	0.082**	(0.014)	0.066**	(0.008)	0.058**	(0.007)
Female headed household (=1)	0.036	(0.091)	-0.143**	(0.047)	-0.096*	(0.043)
Asset index	-0.070**	(0.022)	-0.167**	(0.011)	-0.156**	(0.011)
BMI of mother	-0.038**	(0.008)	-0.076**	(0.004)	-0.062**	(0.004)
BMI^2/100 of mother	0.008	(0.082)	0.020	(0.061)	0.028	(0.052)
Mother has sec. education (=1)	-0.224**	(0.055)	-0.272**	(0.026)	-0.233**	(0.025)
Health facility index (global)	-0.353**	(0.022)	-0.221**	(0.013)	-0.202**	(0.012)
Sec. education in cluster (%)	-0.463*	(0.182)	-1.136**	(0.089)	-1.076**	(0.084)
Child. w. fever in cluster (%)	0.083	(0.190)	-0.364**	(0.100)	-0.380**	(0.095)
Public infras. index	-0.007	(0.023)	-0.008	(0.011)	-0.004	(0.011)
Region fixed effects						
Sub-Saharan Africa (=1)	0.664**	(0.080)	-0.363**	(0.126)	-0.411**	(0.074)
Region interaction effects						
SSA * household size	-0.070**	(0.015)	-0.070**	(0.008)	-0.065**	(0.008)
SSA * female headed hh	-0.140	(0.121)	0.097	(0.070)	-0.034	(0.066)
SSA * vaccination	0.409**	(0.116)	0.329**	(0.077)	0.176*	(0.069)
SSA * first born	-0.109*	(0.111)	0.054	(0.072)	0.091	(0.067)
SSA * preceding birth int.	-0.004	(0.002)	-0.002	(0.001)	-0.001	(0.001)
SSA * breastfeeding	-0.342**	(0.077)	-0.013	(0.045)	-0.003	(0.042)
SSA * asset index (global)	0.002	(0.066)	-0.094*	(0.046)	-0.152**	(0.042)
SSA * mothers' BMI	-0.036**	(0.032)	0.008	(0.008)	0.004	(0.007)
SSA * health facility index	-0.127**	(0.062)	-0.055	(0.043)	0.001	(0.040)
SSA * sec. education (%)	0.008	(0.306)	0.335*	(0.192)	0.510**	(0.174)
SSA * children w. fever (%)	0.140	(0.232)	0.081	(0.139)	0.110	(0.130)
SSA * infras. index (global)	0.044	(0.040)	-0.030	(0.027)	-0.037	(0.025)
R^2	0.110		0.125		0.110	
Obs.	49572		55914		60018	

Source: Demographic and Health Surveys (DHS); own calculations.
Notes: *P-value<0.1. **P-value<0.01. The variables 'age' and 'age^2' denote the age of the mother in the child mortality regression and the age of the child in the two undernutrition regressions. For more details on the variables, see Section 3.3.1.

Essay 4

A Human Development Index by Income Groups

Abstract: One of the most often heard critiques of the HDI is that is does not take into account inequality within countries in its three dimensions. We suggest a relatively easy and intuitive approach which allows to compute the three components and the overall HDI for quintiles of the income distribution. This allows to compare the level in human development of the poor with the level of the non-poor within countries, but also across countries. An empirical illustration for a sample of 14 low and middle income countries shows that inequality in human development within countries is indeed high. The results also show that the level of inequality is not directly linked to the level of human development itself.

based on joint work with Michael Grimm, Kenneth Harttgen and Stephan Klasen.

4.1   Introduction

The Human Development Index (HDI) is a composite index that measures the average achievement in a country in three basic dimensions of human development: a long and healthy life, as measured by life expectancy at birth; knowledge, as measured by the adult literacy rate and the combined gross enrollment ratio for primary, secondary and tertiary schools; and a decent standard of living, as measured by GDP per capita in purchasing power parity US dollars (UNDP, 2006). Based on available statistics UNDP was able to provide an HDI for 177 countries in the latest Human Development Report (UNDP, 2006). The HDI is today widely used in academia, the media and in policy circles to measure and compare progress in human development between countries and over time.

Despite its popularity, which is among other things due to its transparency and simplicity, the HDI is criticized for several reasons.[1] First, it neglects several other dimensions of human well-being, such as for example human rights, security and political participation (see e.g. Anand and Sen (1992), Ranis, Stewart and Samman (2006)). Second, it implies substitution possibilities between the three dimension indices, e.g. a decline in life expectancy can be off set by a rise in GDP per capita.[2] Related to that critique is the third point, which charges that the HDI uses an arbitrary weighting scheme (see e.g. Kelley (1991), Srinivasan (1994) and Ravallion (1997)). For instance, why should education be worth as much as income or health? Finally and fourth, the HDI is often criticized because it only looks at average achievements and, thus, does not take into account the distribution of human development within a country (see e.g. Sagar and Najam (1998)).

When constructing distribution-sensitive measures of human development, limited data availability on the distribution of human development achievements seriously constrains the analysis. Household income surveys are today widely undertaken and, hence provide data on income distribution, but it is much more difficult to get data on inequality in life-expectancy, educational achievements and literacy. Inequality in these dimensions seems, at least in developing countries, also to be very high. There is also broad empirical evidence that mortality as well as educational attainment vary with income and wealth in both rich and poor countries (see e.g. Cutler, Deaton and Lleras-Muney (2006) and Filmer and Pritchett (1999)).

In the past several attempts have been made to integrate inequality into the human development index. Anand and Sen (1992) and Hicks (1997) suggested to discount each dimension index by one minus the Gini coefficient for that dimension before the arithmetic mean over all three is taken. Therefore, high inequality

---

[1]For a critical review, see e.g. Sagar and Najam (1998).

[2]Moreover, if poor people face higher mortality, their deaths would increase per capita incomes of the survivors, generating a further distortion, particularly in HDI trends over time.

in one dimension lowers the index value for that dimension and, hence its contribution to the HDI. Although the idea of such a discount factor is rather intuitive, the Gini-corrected HDI has not been widely used.[3] One reason might be that it is not easy to compute the Gini coefficient for education and life-expectancy due to data limitations and conceptual problems. Another reason might be that it is not clear how to interpret the interaction between the Gini coefficient and the average achievement in a component.

The gender related development index, or GDI, was another attempt in that direction. Its motivation was the 1995 Human Development Report's emphasis on gender inequalities. The GDI adjusts the HDI downward by existing gender inequalities in life-expectancy, education and incomes. The GDI calculates each dimension index separately for men and women and then combines both by taking the harmonic mean, penalizing differences in achievement between men and women. The overall GDI is then calculated by combining the three gender-adjusted dimension indices by taking the arithmetic mean. This concept could of course also be applied using other segmentation variables than gender, such as different ethnic or income groups. However for gender in particular, it is not clear how gender related inequality in income can reasonably be measured.[4] In most cases men and women pool incomes in households. Usually not much information is available how the pooled income is then allocated among household members. That and other critical issues related to the GDI are discussed in detail by Klasen (2006a, 2006b).

Another attempt was undertaken by Foster, López-Calva and Székely (2003). They chose an axiomatic approach to derive a distribution sensitive HDI. They suggest a three-step procedure. First, each dimension index is calculated on the lowest possible aggregation level, given the data availability. For instance, income at the level of households and life-expectancy at the level of municipalities (taken from census data). Second, for each dimension an overall index is computed by taking the generalized mean μ_q. The formula for the generalized mean is $\mu_q = \left[(x_1^q + \ldots + x_n^q)/n\right]^{1/q}$. For $q = 1$, μ yields the arithmetic mean, but for negative values for q, μ gives more emphasis on lower levels of x. The higher the absolute value of q, the more weight is given to low levels of x. Third, the overall HDI is computed by taking again the generalized mean instead of the simple arithmetic mean. The advantage of this approach is its axiomatic foundation. For instance, the index is decomposable by sub-groups, which is not the case for the Gini-corrected HDI. The problem with this approach is, however, that the generalized mean may not seem very intuitive for many users of the HDI. It obviously also

---

[3]See Grün and Klasen (2006) for an analysis of a Gini-adjusted GDP measure.

[4]Generally, the GDI uses information on earned income of males and females, based on sex-specific labor force participation rates and earnings differentials (UNDP, 2006).

raises the question of how to determine the 'right' inequality aversion parameter q. An additional problem is, that again no generally applicable methodology is suggested, which could help to compute the three dimension indices on the lowest disaggregation level.

The approach chosen in this paper differs from the others in that, first, we focus of inequality in human development across the income distribution and, second, we do not try to incorporate the aggregate well-being costs associated with existing inequalities, but rather generate a separate HDI for different segments of the income distribution. More precisely, we take household income and demographic data to compute the three dimension indices for quintiles of the income distribution. This allows on the one hand to track the progress in human development separately for 'the poor' and 'non-poor' and on the other hand to compare the level of human development of the poor to the level of the average population and the level of the non-poor. In contrast to previous attempts, we also present, at least for developing countries, a clear methodology how the three dimension indices for different segments of the income distribution can be calculated with commonly available data sources. Applying our methodology to developed countries entails some data availability and comparability problems which we discuss below. Due to these problems, we are only able to provide rough estimates for two developed countries.

The objective of this paper is first of all illustrative. We will show that our methodology has also some shortcomings, and, hence, all presented results should be interpreted with caution and in the light of our assumptions. The reminder of this paper is organized as follows. Section 2 presents our methodology. Section 3 presents the sample of countries for which we illustrate it. Section 4 discusses the results. Section 5 offers a critical assessment of our methodology. Section 6 concludes.

4.2 Methodology

4.2.1 General idea and overview

The basic idea of our method is to use disaggregated data to calculate the three dimension indices which constitute the HDI for different segments of the income distribution. This will allow us to get an idea of the heterogeneity and inequality in human development which exists within a country. As data sources, we use household surveys. As segments of the income distribution, we define income quintiles.

Since the early nineties, two types of surveys are undertaken in almost all developing countries. First, there are so-called *Living Standard Measurement*

Surveys (LSMS) or a lighter version of it called *Priority Surveys* (PS). Even in countries were none of these two surveys are available, there exist normally at least some other type of living standard survey. These surveys provide, apart from information on household and individual characteristics, data on educational achievement, school enrollment and household income or household expenditure. In what follows, we call this type of survey simply 'household income survey' or 'HIS'. Second, there are so called 'Demographic and Health Surveys' or 'DHS' in short. These surveys are undertaken by the *Macro International Inc., Calverton, Maryland* (usually in cooperation with local authorities and funded by USAID) and provide among other things detailed information on child mortality, health, and fertility. How to proceed for industrialized countries, where usually other types of surveys are undertaken, will be discussed later.

Hence, we will use the HIS to calculate the quintile specific education and GDP indices and the DHS to calculate the quintile specific life expectancy index. The main problems in proceeding so, are that both surveys do not interview the same households (or if so, these households can at least not be matched) and that the DHS does not contain any information on household income or household expenditure, i.e. it is not possible to sort directly the DHS households and individuals by income quintiles.

To solve this problem, we use a simple variant of so-called data matching techniques. The principle of this technique is to estimate the correlation between income and a set of household characteristics which are available in the HIS and the DHS and then to use this correlation pattern to predict income for the households covered by the DHS. However, given that the quality of such a matching process depends heavily on the data quality and data consistency of both types of surveys, we present a second and alternative approach where we use a so-called 'asset index' as segmentation variable. This measure is often used to get an idea of the living standard of households interviewed in the DHS.

Once the three dimension indices are calculated, we simply calculate the quintile specific HDI, which we name QHDI, by taking the arithmetic average of the three dimension indices. In what follows, each step of our method is explained in detail.

4.2.2 Imputing income for DHS households

A regression based approach

The first approach we present is similar to that used in the poverty mapping literature (see e.g. Elbers, Lanjouw and Lanjouw (2003)).[5] The HIS provides infor-

---

[5]Grosse, Klasen and Spatz (2005) recently also used such a technique to match HIS and DHS data for Bolivia.

mation about household income and/or household expenditure. If income is used, the aggregate should contain earned (e.g. wages and profits) as well as unearned income (e.g. transfers). If expenditures are used, the aggregate should contain the expenditure for all items purchased plus the value of the self-produced consumption. According to usual practice in poverty analysis (see e.g. Deaton and Zaidi (2002) expenditures on durables should be excluded. For house owners, hypothetical rents should be imputed. Regional variations in the cost of living should be eliminated using appropriate price deflators. Once the welfare aggregate is calculated, we divide it by household size to receive a per capita measure. We do not use any particular equivalence scale to ensure consistency with the general HDI, which also uses a per capita measure for the income index. In what follows, our per capita welfare measure is denoted y_h, where the index h stands for households $h = 1, \ldots, K$.

Once, y_h is calculated, a common set of variables Ω_h in the HIS and the DHS has to be identified. The variables of Ω have to be correlated with y_h and should at least contain (i) some characteristics of the household head such as age and educational achievement, (ii) characteristics of the household like the number of children, the number of male and female adults in working age and regional variables (such as urban vs. rural, region or province of residence), and (iii) housing conditions like materials of the floor, the roof and the walls, type of electricity and water connection and possibly the number of rooms per person.

Once all these variables are calculated, y_h is regressed in logarithmic form on this set of variables using OLS estimators:

$$\ln y_h^{HIS} = \beta^{HIS} \Omega^{HIS} + u_h, \tag{4.1}$$

where β^{HIS} is a vector of parameters and u_h is the residual.

Using the vector of estimated parameters $\hat{\beta}^{HIS}$, hypothetical incomes for the households covered by the DHS can be calculated by:

$$\hat{\ln y_h}^{DHS} = \hat{\beta}^{HIS} \Omega^{DHS}. \tag{4.2}$$

Given that regressions as in Equation (4.1) rarely explain more than half or three quarter of the total variance in $\ln y_h$, one could generate residuals to account for the unobserved determinants of y_h. We think that would be important, when the objective was to calculate any inequality measure. However, given our objective, we think it is sufficient to assume that the included variables contain enough information on the true income quintile and that in contrast hypothetical residuals may well preserve the natural variance in the data, but at the price of a higher probability of missclasifications over income quintiles.[6] One may also argue that drawing residuals would help to prevent ties, i.e. that households with an identical set Ω will have the same imputed income. However, if Ω is large enough and contains also continuous variables that problem will not arise.

Once the hypothetical incomes for the DHS are imputed, it is possible for both surveys to calculate the cumulative distribution functions of income (person weighted) $F(\ln y_h^{HIS})$ and $F(\ln \hat{y}_h^{DHS})$. Using these distributions it can be determined for each household in which income quintile ($Q = 1, 2, ..., 5$) it is situated.

However, what could pose a problem is, first, that household expenditure may in some cases not be a good proxy of permanent income due to measurement error and limited possibilities of households to smooth consumption, and, second that in some cases the comparability of the HIS and DHS is not high enough, and, hence predicted incomes in a DHS give a biased impression of the distribution of income. Therefore, we present, as mentioned above, a second alternative to classify households in the DHS by income quintile which is based on an asset index approach.

An asset index based approach

In order to construct an asset index for DHS households, first, a set of household assets has to be identified. We suggest the ownership of a radio, TV, refrigerator, bicycle, motorized vehicle, floor material of housing, type of toilet, type of water source and some other assets depending on the country. Second, these assets have to be aggregated into one single metric index for each household using principal component analysis, or, alternatively, the closely related factor analysis (see Filmer and Pritchett (2001) and Sahn and Stifel (2000, 2003)). We used principal component analysis. Once the asset index is built, one can construct, similar to the regression-approach, the cumulative distribution function of the asset index and, hence, households in the DHS can be classified into asset quintiles. Under the assumption that the ownership of assets is a good proxy for income, it can be assumed that the asset quintiles yield a consistent classification to that obtained via observed income in the HIS. Hence, in that case matching between both surveys using these quintiles is possible.

We will use both approaches, the regression based approach and the asset index approach. In principle, the regression based approach is to be favored as income is one of the three components of the HDI and therefore it is consistent to use that approach. Moreover the asset index is sometimes biased, because it

---

[6]Moreover, when imputing residuals for the DHS households, one would in addition have to take into account that the HIS and DHS have generally different sample sizes and a different regional stratification. Hence, the unobserved determinants of y_h will not be distributed identically (see Elbers, Lanjouw and Lanjouw, 2002).

reflects not correctly differences in income between rural and urban areas, due to usually huge differences in prices and the supply of such assets as well as differences in preferences for assets between both areas. On the other hand, the income regression approach yields biased results whenever the distribution of explanatory variables in the regression is not consistent in the HIS and DHS, due either to measurement error or due to different definitions of the variables used in both surveys. As will be shown below, we suspect such a problem to exist particularly in some very poor African countries, and hence in this case it might be that the asset index is a better predictor of true income in these circumstances than predicted income using the estimated regression.

4.2.3   Calculating the life expectancy index by income quintiles

To calculate a life expectancy index by income quintile we combine information on child mortality with model life tables. As mentioned above, the HIS provides usually no information on mortality. The DHS provides only information on child mortality, but not on mortality by all age groups, which would be necessary to construct a life table and to calculate life expectancy directly.

In a first step, we calculate under one child mortality rates by income quintile. To do this we use the information on all children born in the five years preceding the survey. For each child i we calculate the survival time S_i expressed in months m and the survival status d_i. The status variable takes the value one if the child died at the end of S_i and the value zero, if the child was still alive at the age of one. Then we use a simple non-parametric life table estimator to estimate the survival probability for each month after birth, p_m. Through cumulative multiplication we derive for each income quintile the under one mortality rate q_1:

$$q_1^Q = 1 - \prod_{m=1}^{12} p_m^Q, \tag{4.3}$$

We also estimate q_1 over the whole sample, to be able to construct the aggregate life expectancy index.

In a next step, we use the estimated mortality rate q_1 and Ledermann model life tables to calculate quintile specific life expectancy. Ledermann (1969) used historical mortality data for many countries and periods to estimate the relationship between life-expectancy and age-specific mortality rates. He found the following relationship (note that the log function uses the basis 10):

$$\log \hat{q}_j = \hat{a}_{j,0} + \hat{a}_{j,1} \log(100 - e_0), \tag{4.4}$$

where $\hat{q}_j$ is the predicted mortality rate for the age group j, e_0 is the life expectancy at birth and $\hat{a}_{j,0}$ and $\hat{a}_{j,1}$ are the estimated regression coefficients by Ledermann. Ledermann considered age groups defined over five-year intervals, except for the first age group, which he divided into children zero to one year old and one to five years old. In principle, we could also use the Princeton model life tables (Coale and Demeny, 1983), but the problem with those tables is, that first they use not e_0 but e_{10} as entry, i.e. life expectancy at the age of 10. Obviously, it is easier to estimate e_{10} given the probably higher measurement error in child mortality, but to construct the QHDI we need e_0 not e_{10}. Second, Princeton tables end already at a life expectancy of 75 years. Third, Princeton tables are defined separately for men and women, and, hence we would need to estimate child mortality rates separately for boys and girls. This would reduce the number of death events in each income quintile to extremely low levels and therefore lead to very unstable life expectancy estimates. We checked however, whether our life expectancy estimates were consistent with those one would obtain using the Princeton Life Tables 'West'. That was the case, and, hence, we are confident that our Lederman approach yields acceptable results. However, a drawback of both types of tables—Ledermann and Princeton—is that their estimation included almost no countries of today's developing world and no countries affected by the AIDS epidemic. In particular the latter omission might be problematic, given that AIDS usually affects strongly the age-mortality pattern by increasing mortality among children below the age of 5 (through mother-child transmission) and mortality among adults in age of activity.

To calculate quintile specific life expectancy, we take the inverse of Equation (4.4) and the regression coefficients for the age group 1 year old:

$$\hat{e}_0^Q = 100 - \left[\frac{q_1^Q}{10^{\hat{a}_{1,0}}} \right]^{\frac{1}{\hat{a}_{1,1}}} \quad \forall\, Q = 1, 2, \ldots, 5. \tag{4.5}$$

with $\hat{a}_{1,0} = -1.98384$ and $\hat{a}_{1,1} = 2.40372$ (Ledermann, 1969).

Aggregate life expectancy can be calculated using q_1 instead of q_1^Q.

Then we calculate the quintile specific life expectancy index, L^Q, using the usual minimum and maximum values for life expectancy employed to calculate the HDI:

$$L^Q = \frac{\hat{e}_0^Q - 25}{85 - 25} \quad \forall\, Q = 1, 2, \ldots, 5. \tag{4.6}$$

The aggregate life expectancy index L can be calculated using $\hat{e}_0$ instead of $\hat{e}_0^Q$.

In a last step, we rescale linearly L^Q and L to achieve consistency with the aggregate HDI calculated by UNDP. As rescaling factor we use the ratio between our aggregate life expectancy index L and the aggregate life expectancy index calculated by UNDP for the particular year in question. [7] Consistency is not automatic, given that our approach and UNDP's approach are based on different data sources. Given that the objective of our approach is first of all to examine the *distribution* of human development, differences in levels should not present any serious problem.

4.2.4   Calculating the education index by income quintiles

To calculate the quintile specific education index, we use the information on literacy and school enrollment provided by the HIS.

Calculating the adult literacy index

The questions providing information about adult literacy may significantly vary from one HIS to the other. Sometimes adults are simply asked whether they are able to read and write. Other surveys are much more specific in asking whether the person is able to read a newspaper and to write a letter. This is even sometimes directly tested. In addition, in some countries one has to distinguish between having knowledge of any local language or of the official language of the country. Finally in some surveys, such information is completely missing. In this latter case, it is possible to use educational achievement as proxy for literacy. However, it is far from evident to determine after how many years of school a person is literate. This varies a lot from country to country or even within a country (for West-Africa, see e.g. Michaelowa (2001)). We proceeded as follows. If an adult declared to be able to read and/or write in any language (with or without proof), we considered him or her as literate. If that information was not available, we considered somebody as literate if he or she achieved at least a grade which corresponds to five years of schooling. Adults are defined as persons above the age of 15.

Quintile specific adult literacy is then calculated by the following equation:

$$a^Q = \frac{1}{n^Q} \sum_{i(\forall j > 15)} I(a_i^Q > \bar{a}) \quad \forall Q = 1, 2, \dots, 5, \tag{4.7}$$

where n^Q is the total number of adults in quintile Q and I is an indicator function which takes the value one if literacy status of adult i, a_i is over the above defined threshold value $\bar{a}$ and zero otherwise. We calculate also the aggregate adult literacy rate a.

---

[7]If the DHS and HIS are from different years, we re-scale to the later year.

Then we calculate the quintile specific adult literacy index, A^Q, using again the corresponding usual minimum and maximum values employed in the HDI:

$$A^Q = \frac{a^Q - 0}{1 - 0} \quad \forall\, Q = 1, 2, \ldots, 5. \tag{4.8}$$

The aggregate adult literacy index A can be calculated using a instead of a^Q.

In a last step, we rescale again linearly A^Q and A to achieve consistency with the aggregate HDI calculated by UNDP for the relevant year. As rescaling factor we use the ratio between our aggregate literacy index A and the aggregate literacy index calculated by UNDP.

Calculating the enrollment index

To calculate the quintile specific gross enrolment index, we calculate first the combined gross enrolment rate for each quintile. Each individual attending school or university whether general or vocational is considered as enrolled. We define this rate over all individuals of the age group five to 23 years old. Age is for each individual the age at the date of the interview. This yields:

$$g^Q = \frac{1}{n^Q} \sum_{i(\forall 5 \leq j \leq 23)} I(g_i^Q > 0) \quad \forall\, Q = 1, 2, \ldots, 5, \tag{4.9}$$

where n^Q is the total number of individuals of age five to 23 in quintile Q and I is an indicator function which takes the value one if an individual i independent of age, is enrolled, i.e. $g_i > 0$. We calculate also the aggregate gross enrolment rate g.

Then we calculate the quintile specific gross enrollment index, G^Q using the usual minimum and maximum values used for the calculation of the HDI:

$$G^Q = \frac{g^Q - 0}{1 - 0} \quad \forall\, Q = 1, 2, \ldots, 5. \tag{4.10}$$

The aggregate gross enrollment index G can be calculated by using g instead of g^Q. Finally, we also rescale G^Q and G to the level of the HDI enrollment index.

Calculating the education index

The quintile specific education index E^Q is calculated using the same weighted average as the HDI:

$$E^Q = (2/3) \times A^Q + (1/3) \times G^Q \quad \forall\, Q = 1, 2, \ldots, 5. \tag{4.11}$$

The aggregate education index E can be calculated by using A and G instead of A^Q and G^Q.

4.2.5   Calculating the GDP index by income quintiles

To calculate the GDP index by income quintile, we use our income variable from the HIS. One main difference with the two other dimension indices is that mean income calculated from the HIS can be *very* different from GDP per capita derived from National Accounts data, which is used for the GDP index in the general HDI. This has two reasons: first, because of conceptual differences and, second, because of measurement error on both levels. GDP measures the value of all goods and services produced for the market within a year in a given country evaluated at market prices. Income in the household survey is either measured, as mentioned above, via household expenditure (including self-consumed production) or via the sum of earned and unearned household income. Therefore, non distributed profits of enterprises, property income and so on will not be included in the household income variable. Moreover, on the household survey side, there may be measurement errors, because it is difficult to get accurate responses from households concerning wages, profits and expenditures. On the National Accounts side, while supply-side information on output and income for some sectors is based on high-quality surveys or census data for agriculture and industry, information about subsistence farmers and informal producers is harder to obtain and usually of lower quality.[8]

We proceed as follows. First, to eliminate differences in national price levels we express household income per capita y_h calculated from the HIS, in USD PPP using the conversion factors based on price data from the latest International Comparison Program surveys provided by the World Bank (2005):

$$y_h^{PPP} = y_h \times PPP. \qquad (4.12)$$

Second, we rescale y_h^{PPP} using the ratio between $\bar{y}^{PPP}$ and GDP per capita expressed in PPP (taken from the general HDI), i.e. we only take the information on the distribution of income from the HIS and stick with GDP per capita as the level of income:

$$ry_h^{PPP} = y_h^{PPP} \times \left[\frac{GDPPC^{PPP}}{\bar{y}^{PPP}} \right]. \qquad (4.13)$$

---

[8]A detailed discussion of all these problems can be found in Ravallion (2001) and Deaton (2005).

Once, theses adjustments are done, it is straightforward to calculate the quintile specific GDP index, again using the usual minimum and maximum values of the HDI:

$$Y^Q = \frac{\log \bar{r}y^{Q,PPP} - \log(100)}{\log(40,000) - \log(100)} \quad \forall Q = 1,2,\ldots,5, \tag{4.14}$$

where $\bar{r}y^{Q,PPP}$ is the quintile specific arithmetic mean of the rescaled household income per capita.

It should be noted that in richer countries the GDP per capita measure for the richest quintile, $\bar{r}y^{5,PPP}$, could easily exceed 40,000 USD PPP and, hence, the index could take a value greater than 1.

4.2.6 Calculating the overall HDI and the HDI by income quintiles

Once the quintile specific dimension indices have been calculated, determining the QHDI is straightforward. It is the simple average of the three dimension indices:

$$HDI^Q = (1/3) \times L^Q + (1/3) \times E^Q + (1/3) \times Y^Q$$

$$\forall Q = 1,2,\ldots,5. \tag{4.15}$$

The aggregate HDI is as usual given by:

$$HDI = (1/3) \times L + (1/3) \times E + (1/3) \times Y. \tag{4.16}$$

To get a sense of the inequality in human development within a country, one may compute the ratio between the HDI for the richest quintile and the poorest quintile:

$$RQHDI^{5,1} = \frac{HDI^{Q=5}}{HDI^{Q=1}}, \tag{4.17}$$

or the ratio of the quintile specific HDI to the aggregate HDI:

$$RQHDI^{1,mean} = \frac{HDI^{Q=1}}{HDI} \quad \text{and} \quad RQHDI^{5,mean} = \frac{HDI^{Q=5}}{HDI}. \tag{4.18}$$

All these indicators can of course also be calculated for each dimension index. Hence, the QHDI cannot only be used to inform about the level of human development of the poor, the rich and the groups in-between, but also about the inequality in human development within a society. Moreover, the quintile specific indices can be compared across countries. This may lead to results where country A has a higher overall HDI than country B, but that in country B human development of the poor is on a substantial higher level than in country A.

4.2.7   Calculating the HDI by income quintiles for OECD countries

The application of our approach to OECD countries entails some additional problems. The data availability is very different in developing and industrialized countries. Whereas for a long time access to disaggregated and harmonized income, education and health data was much better in industrialized countries than in developing countries is seems today to be the other way around. For many developing countries there exist today at least roughly comparable income, education and health data thanks to the household income surveys and Demographic and Health Surveys. In many industrialized countries, such standardized surveys are either absent or not easily accessible. Moreover, due to very low infant and child mortality levels in rich countries, we could not easily apply our methods of deducing life expectancy from infant or child mortality rates available in household survey data as the absolute number of infant and child deaths are too low in such surveys to calculate life expectancies (and its differential by income) with any reliability. Thus we will briefly discuss data availability and outline an approach to construct quintile-specific HDIs in rich countries and illustrate it for Finland and the USA. However, these calculations are not fully comparable to the calculations for developing countries and thus should be viewed as tentative.

Matters are easiest for the income component. Here we can rely on the Luxemburg Income Study (LIS), which produces harmonized micro data sets on income, demographics, labor market status and expenditures on the level of households and individuals for 30 OECD countries.[9] These data are of very high quality and probable more reliable than the income/expenditure data available in many developing countries. For our examples, Finland and the USA, we took the LIS income data for the year 2000 and simply rescaled it to fit UNDP's GDP index.

Unfortunately, the data sets contained in LIS do not have educational enrolment or adult literacy information and only provide information on educational achievements by levels of education passed. Therefore, for Finland and the USA, we assume no inequality in adult literacy and use the schooling achievement differential by income for 2000 as reported in the Luxembourg Income Study to estimate income differentials in enrolments, after which we rescale again. Alternatively, enrolment rates by income quintile could probably be generated from national household income surveys (or coordinated surveys such as the European Household Panel Survey) but this would mean that we rely on two different income measures to calculate the two different components (as we had to do with the HIS and the DHS for developing countries).

---

[9]For details see: http://www.lisproject.org.

A different approach would be to use data from the 'International Adult Literacy Survey (IALS)' for the education component. This is an international comparative study designed to provide information about the skills of the adult populations. It was conducted in three phases (1994, 1996 and 1998) in 20 nations.[10] There exists also a follow up survey called 'Adult Literacy and Lifeskills (ALL) Survey' but which exists so far only in six countries. A problem with using that information would be that it is not directly comparable to the literacy and enrolment measures used for all the other countries.

By far the most difficult issues arise however with the life expectancy component. As already stated, using quintile specific child mortality to derive an estimate of quintile specific life expectancy from household surveys would not be possible as child mortality in most OECD countries is so low that no meaningful differentials by income could be identified. Moreover, child mortality in these countries is much related to premature births, genetic defects, complications during birth and due to accidents all of which not closely related to income. In fact, it is likely that existing income differentials in life expectancy in rich countries are largely due to mortality beyond childhood.

In principle, one could try to rely on census or census-like sample surveys with large numbers of observations. An alternative would be to rely on death registrations. These data sources are generally used in rich countries to calculate mortality rates and associated life expectancy statistics. But these data sources usually do not include incomes and cannot be used to calculate income differentials. Two exceptions are the USA and Finland where specialized analyses on the link between incomes and mortality were undertaken. We therefore use the results from Rogot *et al.* (1997) and Martikainen *et al.* (2001) on the life expectancy differential by incomes. These data are based on linked income survey data with vital registration data and are covering the adult mortality experience for 1979-85 for the USA, and 1991-96 for Finland. Through matching the mortality experience by income quintile with the Model Life Tables 'North' (Coale and Demeny, 1983), we derive life expectancy at birth for the two countries, after which we re-scale as described above.[11]

An alternative way would be to use similar data matching techniques that we used above to impute incomes into the DHS to impute incomes into census data and then generate life expectancy information by income quintile. That presupposes access to census data (which are not available or accessible in some countries) and a detailed analysis of the potential of such a method.

---

[10]For details see: http://nces.ed.gov/surveys/all/.

[11]The 'income' that is referred to in these studies does not closely match annual household per capita income that we would use for the income component which causes a further complication. See also discussion below.

Given these caveats, we included only Finland and the USA in our analysis and focus otherwise solely on low and middle income countries and leave the calculation of a QHDI for OECD countries for future work.

4.3 Illustrating sample of countries

Besides Finland and the USA, we illustrate our approach for a sample of 13 developing countries: seven countries from Sub-Saharan Africa (Burkina Faso, Côte d'Ivoire, Cameroon, Guinea, Madagascar, Mozambique, South-Africa and Zambia), three countries from Latin America (Bolivia, Colombia, and Nicaragua), and two countries from South-East Asia (Indonesia and Vietnam). These countries are listed in Table A.1 (Appendix D). We tried to restrict the sample to countries where a HIS and DHS were undertaken within a two-year time period. For two countries both surveys were undertaken in the same year. For three countries there is a gap of one year and for four countries a gap of two years. Only in three countries (Guinea, Indonesia, and Madagascar) we were not able to follow this rule and have actually a gap between both surveys of three to four years. Moreover, we tried to include countries where both surveys are not older than five years. This was however not possible for four countries (Côte d'Ivoire, Guinea, Madagascar, South-Africa), where the HIS or the DHS (or both) were undertaken at the end of the 1990s. The survey dates should also be taken into account when comparing our unscaled QHDI with the usual HDI. The published HDI in the UNDP's Human Development Report 2005 (UNDP, 2005) refers to the year 2003. But a closer look at the data sources shows that literacy rates and life-expectancy estimates were usually based on censuses or surveys conducted between 2000 and 2004. In several countries the data sources even stem from data collected in the 1990s (e.g. Belarus, Burkina Faso, Kazakhstan, Mali). Hence, time consistency between the different dimension indices and actuality of the data is not a problem specific to our approach, but rather is present for both the usual HDI and the QHDI.

4.4 Results

Table 1 shows the HDI by income quintile, the HDI, and the ratio of the HDI for the richest quintile to the poorest quintile and the HDI ranking for the richest and poorest quintile (using the HDI values from the 2005 report) for the sample countries. The countries are sorted by descending HDI. The results reveal very stark differences in human development between the richest and the poorest quintile. For example, in Guinea, Burkina Faso, Zambia, and Madagascar, the HDI for the richest income quintile is about twice as high as in the poorest quintile. In a second group of countries, including Bolivia, Cameroon, Nicaragua, Côte d'Ivoire, Mozambique, and South Africa, the gap between the rich and the poor is also very large, between 50% and 65%. In a third group of countries, comprising Colombia, Vietnam, and Indonesia, the differential in the HDI for the richest and poorest quintile is smaller but still substantial at about 30%-50%. In the two rich countries included, the differences are smaller than in developing countries but large differences remain between the quintiles, particularly in the USA.

The rank positions of the different quintiles further illustrate this point. For example, the richest quintile in Bolivia is at rank 34, i.e. among the countries with high human development, actually at the same level as Poland, whereas the poorest quintile is at rank 132. The average HDI Bolivia was in the last year's report at rank 112. In some Sub-Saharan African countries such as Cameroon, Guinea and Madagascar the richest quintile achieves a level similar to those countries with medium human development, i.e. far above the threshold of 0.5. In contrast the poorest quintiles of these countries all rank among the 15 countries with the lowest HDI. Put differently, the differences within countries are as high as the differences between high and medium as well as medium and low human development countries. Also among rich countries, the differences are sizable. While the richest quintile in the USA (followed by Finland) would top the list of human development achievements, the poorest quintile in the USA only achieves rank 48, considerably worse off than the richest quintile in South Africa, Colombia, Bolivia, or Indonesia. These differences are also nicely illustrated in Figure 4.1.

When examining the individual components (see Tables A.2 A.3, A.4 in Appendix), it becomes clear that the biggest effect of inequality on the quintile-specific HDI is in the income component. As Table A.4 shows, in many countries the richest quintile has an income index (Y) that is often more than twice or even up to five times as high as among the poorest quintile. Here many of the Sub-Saharan African countries have the highest inequality, followed closely by the Latin America while the two East Asian countries have ratios of less than 2. This may seem surprising since it is well-known that Latin American countries have, on average, (slightly) higher income inequality than Sub-Saharan African countries. The reason why this is not reflected here is that the income index uses a logarithmic transformation of incomes under the assumption that the well-being effects of higher incomes among the rich is declining with higher incomes. Thus what is being measured here is not the differential in incomes but, in line with the general treatment of the income component in the HDI, the differential in important aspects of quality of life such as nutrition, housing, clothing, and other aspects that are closely correlated with incomes. In that sense it is particularly worrying that the differential is so stark in Africa and Latin America.

Table 4.1: Quintile specific HDI by country

(L^Q computed using asset index)

Country	$Q=1$	$Q=2$	$Q=3$	$Q=4$	$Q=5$	Overall HDI	Ratio $Q5/Q1$ $Q5/Q1$	Ranking All	Ranking $Q=1$	Ranking $Q=5$
Industrialized Countries										
USA (2000)	0.837	0.893	0.927	0.957	1.011	0.940	1.208	15	48	1
Finland (2000)	0.870	0.897	0.919	0.944	0.989	0.930	1.137	20	32	1
Developing Countries										
Colombia (2003/2005)	0.673	0.741	0.800	0.857	0.927	0.790	1.377	66	115	22
Vietnam (2004/2002)	0.627	0.680	0.718	0.765	0.828	0.713	1.321	108	125	51
Indonesia (2000/2003)	0.593	0.651	0.700	0.764	0.874	0.701	1.474	110	129	31
South Africa (2000/1998)	0.561	0.640	0.700	0.743	0.879	0.691	1.567	112	132	30
Bolivia (2002/2003)	0.550	0.640	0.704	0.741	0.863	0.690	1.570	113	132	34
Nicaragua (2001/2001)	0.531	0.629	0.678	0.720	0.830	0.667	1.563	116	135	51
Cameroon (2001/2004)	0.417	0.477	0.529	0.553	0.644	0.523	1.544	137	165	123
Madagascar (2001/1997)	0.343	0.463	0.496	0.563	0.684	0.488	1.994	152	173	114
Guinea (1995/1999)	0.340	0.457	0.490	0.594	0.696	0.467	2.047	156	174	111
Cote d'Ivoire (1998/1999)	0.343	0.416	0.434	0.515	0.561	0.430	1.636	163	173	132
Zambia (2002/2002)	0.317	0.390	0.431	0.476	0.583	0.426	1.839	164	175	129
Mozambique (2002/2003)	0.305	0.355	0.380	0.417	0.504	0.387	1.652	167	176	146
Burkina Faso (2003/2003)	0.257	0.306	0.331	0.365	0.489	0.348	1.903	172	178	151

Note: For developing countries the years in brackets refer to the respective survey years. The first year refers to the HIS data set, the second to the DHS data set. All indices are rescaled to UNDP's reported HDI value of the second survey year.

Source: Household Income Survey (HIS) and Demographic and Health Surveys (DHS) (see Table A.1), Human Development Reports; calculations by the authors.

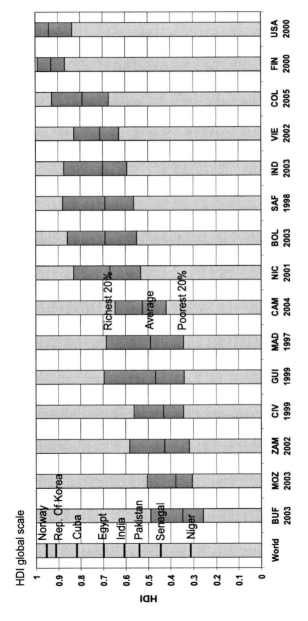

Figure 4.1: A human development index by income groups

Source: Computations by the authors. HDI global scale (HDR 2006).

The differential in educational achievements (E) between the richest and the poorest quintile are also sizable, but smaller than in the income index (see Table A.3). In some Sub-Saharan African countries such as Burkina Faso and Madagascar the rich have nearly twice the educational achievement of the poor. But in many other countries such as South Africa, Vietnam, Nicaragua and Colombia, the differentials are not very large reflecting substantial efforts to improve education across the entire income spectrum. One should note, however, that education is only using literacy and enrolment rates and says little about educational quality which is likely to differ much more strongly between the rich and the poor.

The differential in life expectancy achievements (L) between the richest and poorest quintile are also substantial, but generally the smallest of the three components. In Appendix we present the results for both matching approaches, the income regression based approach (see Table A.2) and the asset index based approach (see Table A2b). While one reason for the smaller inequality in the life-expectancy index compared to the two other dimension indices may be related to data quality issues and the assumptions that were made in order to derive at these estimates (see also Section 4.5), it appears that inequality in life expectancy is indeed smaller in the developing countries we consider than other forms of inequality. Three cautionary notes are important, however. To some extent, such smaller inequality is to be expected given that life expectancy is effectively bounded above, i.e. there are limits to life expectancy that even high income people run up against. Second, the differences in actual life expectancy (rather than the life expectancy index) are still substantial with gaps between the poorest and richest quintile amounting to more than 10 years in 5 countries. Third, even seemingly smaller differentials in life expectancy may be seen as just as important, or even more important, than larger differentials in the other components. After all, the chance to live and be free from the fear of premature mortality is a fundamental precondition for all other aspects of life.

Among rich countries, all three differentials are considerably smaller. Income differentials (especially when expressed using the logarithmic transformation) are considerably smaller suggesting smaller differentials in income-sensitive human development achievements than elsewhere. Education differentials are, as expected, also smaller as schooling up to secondary level and thus basic literacy is near universal and only slight differentials exist at the post-secondary level. Also life expectancy differentials by income (based on cause of death information for the 1980s or early 1990s) are smaller in developing countries but remain sizable. In both the USA and Finland, the top quintiles enjoys about five more years of life than the poorest quintile. Given the wealth of these countries and the ability to provide health case to all, such differentials seem still unacceptably large.

The correlation between the level of the HDI and inequality in human development seems to be negative but only weakly so as Figure 4.2 illustrates.

Figure 4.2: Correlation between the overall HDI and the ratio between the QHDI for the richest and the poorest quintile

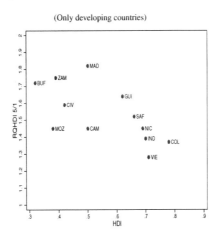

Source: Computations by the authors.

4.5 Limits of the approach

Computing an index of well-being for different income groups is a serious challenge. The exercise is first of all constrained by data availability. In addition there is clearly a trade-off between transparency, simplicity and an intuitive interpretation on the one hand and accuracy and computational complexity on the other hand. In our approach we rather tried to elaborate an index which is relatively transparent, simple to calculate and easy to interpret. In consequence, we were forced to make many simplifications. The most important ones are discussed in what follows. Hence, the paper should first of all be seen as an illustrative exercise, which hopefully enhances the discussion and sensitizes policy makers for inequality in human development within countries. But it should not be seen by economists and demographers as an attempt to reflect accurately and exactly inequality and income differentials in health and education.

First, our segmentation variable, household income, has obviously a different temporal dimension than our indicators for life expectancy and education. Household income as measured in household surveys is clearly a period estimate, even if it is approximated by household expenditure, which could be seen as a rough measure of permanent income. Hence, assuming that people stay at this level throughout life, which is implicitly done the way we use it, is probably false and is likely to overstate income inequality. Whether this also leads to an overestimation in the income differentials of life expectancy and education is unclear. However, if such a bias exists, it would at least partly be offset by a bias in the opposite direction: If the difference between permanent income and period income is mainly driven by age and if education and life expectancy are higher among younger cohorts, then the education and life expectancy differentials by income are underestimated.

This leads directly to the second problematic point. In industrialized countries, where education at least up to some grade and basic health provision is provided costless to everyone, income differentials in health and education may to a large extent be driven by preferences. However, this is certainly less the case for developing countries, where health and education are often very costly. Hence, the QHDI we suggest, might have a very different interpretation in industrialized and developing countries.

Third, the matching method we use to impute incomes for the DHS is, as mentioned above, based on a couple of strong assumptions. Among other things, we assume that the distribution of unobservable factors is the same in both surveys and uncorrelated with income. Both assumptions are certainly not met and, hence, life expectancy is not exactly calculated for the same quintiles of households than education and average income.

Fourth, as the results show it is hard to get precise estimates of the human development index for very poor countries. This is on the one hand due to the general lower quality of data in poor countries and on the other hand in particular due to the difficulty to derive reliable estimates of life expectancy. This can be seen by inspection of Table A.2. The life expectancy index decreases in some countries when going from a poorer quintile to a richer quintile (e.g. Burkina Faso, Guinea, Mozambique), in particular when the income regression based approach is used for computation. Several explanations might be invoked. Given that we derived life expectancy from survey based estimates of child mortality, the potential measurement error is obviously high, due to in some cases rather small sample sizes and potentially very imprecise household's declarations regarding the death date of their children. These errors might themselves be correlated with income. The life table approach introduces an additional bias given that the used tables do not account for AIDS specific age-mortality patterns. Moreover, as already mentioned above, the suggested method to match data from the HIS and the DHS by income quintile might pose problems when the data quality is limited. This is in particular the case in some of the African countries. For instance, when the set of common variables Ω is rather small or when the distribution of the variables included in Ω differs in both surveys. This may arise if the variable definitions are not exactly the same in both surveys. Or if interviewers coded the answers not exactly identically, although the questions have been asked in exactly the same way. However, the usual aggregate estimates are, at least to some extent, also affected by these problems and hence there is also uncertainty regarding the general HDI in these countries.

4.6 Conclusion

One of the most often heard critiques of the HDI is that this index does not take into account inequality in its three dimensions within countries. We suggested a relatively easy, transparent and intuitive approach which allows to compute the three dimension indices and the overall HDI for quintiles of the income distribution. This allows to compare the level in human development of the poor with the level of the non-poor within and across countries. The illustration for a sample of 13 low and middle income countries, as well as 2 rich countries showed that inequality in human development within countries is indeed high. The results also showed that the level of inequality is only weakly linked to the level of human development itself. Therefore, this information is not yet contained in the overall HDI.

The implementation of our approach is obviously more time consuming and data demanding than the calculation of the usual HDI. However the necessary data—a Household Income Survey and a Demographic and Health Survey—exists now in at least most of the low and middle income countries. As discussed above, for industrialized countries getting harmonized data on education and life expectancy differentials is surprisingly a bit more problematic.

Of course our approach is not without its limits. This was discussed in detail in the previous section. However, we think it can make a useful contribution to the measurement of human development and should sensitize policy makers to inequality not only in income but also in education and life expectancy which are without any doubt two important determinants of individual well-being.

Appendix A

Table A.1: Poverty/Growth elasticity as a function of mean income and income inequality(assumption: no change in distribution)

Gini	Poverty line as a proportion of mean income									
	0.10	0.20	0.30	0.40	0.50	0.60	0.70	0.80	0.90	1.00
0.20	17.86	12.63	9.63	7.57	6.02	4.82	3.85	3.07	2.43	1.92
0.25	11.26	8.00	6.16	4.89	3.95	3.22	2.64	2.17	1.78	1.46
0.30	7.67	5.48	4.25	3.42	2.80	2.32	1.94	1.63	1.37	1.16
0.35	5.51	3.96	3.09	2.51	2.08	1.75	1.48	1.27	1.09	0.94
0.40	4.09	2.96	2.33	1.91	1.60	1.36	1.17	1.02	0.89	0.78
0.45	3.13	2.27	1.81	1.49	1.26	1.08	0.94	0.83	0.73	0.65
0.50	2.43	1.78	1.42	1.18	1.01	0.88	0.77	0.68	0.61	0.55
0.55	1.91	1.41	1.13	0.95	0.82	0.03	0.63	0.56	0.51	0.46
0.60	1.51	1.12	0.91	0.77	0.66	0.58	0.52	0.47	0.43	0.39
0.65	1.20	0.89	0.73	0.62	0.54	0.48	0.43	0.39	0.35	0.32
0.70	0.95	0.71	0.58	0.50	0.44	0.39	0.35	0.32	0.29	0.27

Table A.2: Poverty/Distribution change elasticity as a function of mean income and income inequality(assumption: no change in distribution)

Gini	Poverty line as a proportion of mean income								
	0.20	0.30	0.40	0.50	0.60	0.70	0.80	0.90	1.00
0.20	58.99	34.10	20.71	12.73	7.73	4.52	2.46	1.15	0.34
0.25	30.39	17.83	11.05	6.97	4.38	2.68	1.56	0.82	0.33
0.30	17.69	10.56	6.68	4.32	2.81	1.80	1.11	0.64	0.32
0.35	11.20	6.80	4.39	2.92	1.95	1.30	0.85	0.53	0.30
0.40	7.53	4.65	3.07	2.09	1.44	1.00	0.68	0.45	0.29
0.45	5.29	3.33	2.25	1.57	1.11	0.80	0.57	0.40	0.27
0.50	3.85	2.47	1.70	1.22	0.89	0.65	0.48	0.36	0.26
0.55	2.87	1.88	1.32	0.97	0.04	0.55	0.42	0.32	0.25
0.60	2.18	1.46	1.05	0.78	0.60	0.47	0.37	0.29	0.23
0.65	1.68	1.15	0.84	0.64	0.50	0.40	0.32	0.26	0.21
0.70	1.30	0.91	0.68	0.53	0.42	0.34	0.28	0.24	0.20

Table A.3: Theoretical values of headcount poverty as a function of mean income and income inequality(assumption: no change in distribution)

Gini	Poverty line as a proportion of mean income								
	0.20	0.30	0.40	0.50	0.60	0.70	0.80	0.90	1.00
0.20	0.00	0.07	0.87	3.96	10.63	20.71	32.86	45.43	57.11
0.25	0.04	0.72	3.53	9.46	18.19	28.56	39.36	49.66	58.91
0.30	0.37	2.64	7.94	15.88	25.30	35.12	44.55	53.15	60.74
0.35	1.44	5.99	13.41	22.38	31.73	40.71	48.93	56.22	62.58
0.40	3.60	10.52	19.36	28.64	37.52	45.62	52.79	59.05	64.46
0.45	6.93	15.83	25.42	34.56	42.80	50.03	56.31	61.72	66.37
0.50	11.31	21.62	31.43	40.14	47.66	54.10	59.60	64.30	68.33
0.55	16.54	27.67	37.31	45.44	98.65	57.94	62.75	66.84	70.34
0.60	22.45	33.85	43.06	50.51	56.59	61.62	65.82	69.38	72.41
0.65	28.88	40.13	48.71	55.43	60.81	65.21	68.86	71.94	74.56
0.70	35.75	46.47	54.29	60.26	64.96	68.78	71.93	74.57	76.82

Table A.4: Poverty/Distribution change semi-elasticity as a function of mean income and inequality(assumption: zero growth of mean income)

	Poverty line as a proportion of mean income									
Gini	0.10	0.20	0.30	0.40	0.50	0.60	0.70	0.80	0.90	1.00
0.20	0.00	0.00	0.02	0.18	0.50	0.82	0.94	0.81	0.52	0.20
0.25	0.00	0.01	0.13	0.39	0.66	0.80	0.77	0.61	0.41	0.19
0.30	0.00	0.06	0.28	0.53	0.69	0.71	0.63	0.49	0.34	0.19
0.35	0.01	0.16	0.41	0.59	0.65	0.62	0.53	0.41	0.30	0.19
0.40	0.04	0.27	0.49	0.59	0.60	0.54	0.45	0.36	0.27	0.19
0.45	0.10	0.37	0.53	0.57	0.54	0.48	0.40	0.32	0.25	0.18
0.50	0.18	0.43	0.53	0.53	0.49	0.42	0.35	0.29	0.23	0.18
0.55	0.27	0.47	0.52	0.49	0.44	0.04	0.32	0.26	0.21	0.17
0.60	0.35	0.49	0.49	0.45	0.39	0.34	0.29	0.24	0.20	0.17
0.65	0.40	0.49	0.46	0.41	0.35	0.30	0.26	0.22	0.19	0.16
0.70	0.44	0.47	0.42	0.37	0.32	0.27	0.24	0.20	0.18	0.15

Table A.5: Descriptives of Regions

Region	Headcount poverty	Headcount poverty (theo.)	Gini Coeff.	Mean Income	P0 relative growth	P0 absolute growth	Income growth	Gini growth
East Asia and Pacific	16.46	20.68	39.74	1105	-3.45	-7.93	11.48	2.53
Europe and Central Asia	2.47	2.55	29.41	2235	1.70	220.04	-12.97	18.20
Latin America and Caribbean	14.77	16.26	51.47	2011	-0.14	47.92	3.10	0.96
Middle East and North Africa	1.93	4.74	37.44	1909	-0.16	-11.43	-9.14	-8.16
South Asia	34.35	32.09	32.44	646	-1.68	-1.04	3.92	4.20
Sub-Saharan Africa	35.88	34.51	43.20	900	2.39	21.10	-7.08	-0.76

Appendix B

Figure A.1: Stunting/Wasting Combinations for Underweight of -2.0

(WHO reference standard)

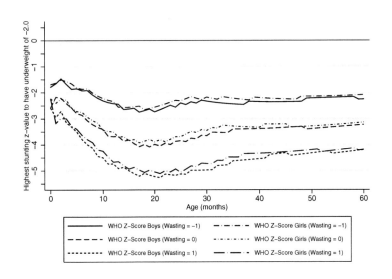

Source: WHO and NCHS/WHO reference standard; own calculations.

Figure A.2: Stunting/Wasting Combinations for Underweight of -2.0

(NCHS/WHO reference standard)

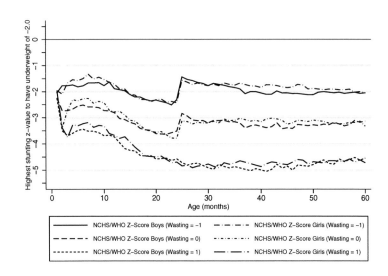

Source: WHO and NCHS/WHO reference standard; own calculations.

Figure A.3: Composition of undernutrition in Burkina Faso by asset index quintiles

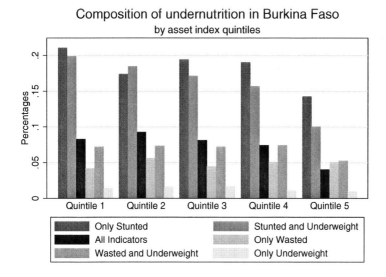

Source: DHS dataset (Burkina Faso 2003); own calculations.

Figure A.4: Composition of undernutrition in Bolivia by asset index quintiles

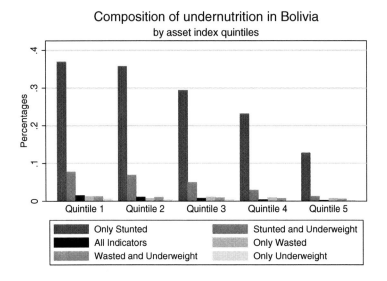

Source: DHS dataset (Bolivia 2003); own calculations.

Figure A.5: Composition of undernutrition in Chad by the nutrition status of
mother

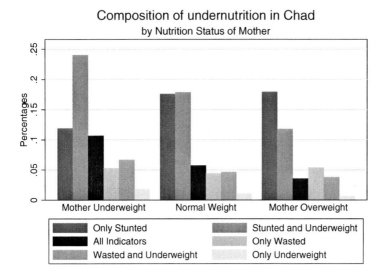

Source: DHS dataset (Chad 2003); own calculations.

Figure A.6: Composition of undernutrition in India by the nutrition status of mother

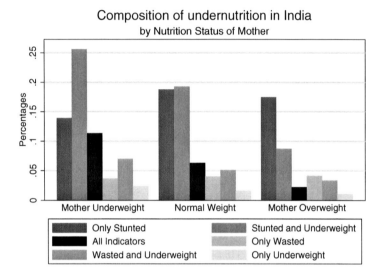

Source: DHS dataset (India 1998/99); own calculations.

Appendix C

Table A.1: Scoring Coefficients
for Asset Index and Access to Health Facilities Index
(Principal Component Analysis)

	Bangla-desh 2000	India 1999	Mali 2001	Uganda 1995	Zim-babwe 1994	Global value
Asset index						
Radio	0.191	0.173	0.135	0.173	0.141	0.221
TV	0.284	0.270	0.272	0.245	0.195	0.332
Fridge	–	0.239	0.249	0.182	0.167	–
Bike	0.093	0.077	0.021	-0.002	0.036	0.095
Motorized transport	0.143	0.229	0.205	0.177	0.128	0.263
Low floor material	-0.300	–	-0.255	-0.274	-0.184	–
No toilet facility	-0.125	-0.265	-0.144	-0.118	-0.172	-0.220
Flush toilet	0.273	0.282	0.105	0.195	0.221	0.308
Piped drinking water	0.192	0.196	0.206	0.243	0.203	0.268
Surface drinking water	-0.048	-0.070	-0.085	-0.143	-0.086	-0.142
Access to health facility index						
Tetanus vaccination	0.393	0.349	0.344	0.480	0.403	0.358
Prenatal care	0.450	0.367	0.347	0.487	0.442	0.376
Born w/o assistance	-0.357	-0.312	-0.335	-0.252	-0.307	-0.286

Source: Demographic and Health Surveys (DHS); own calculations.

Table A.2: Regression Results of Infant Mortality (Logistic Regression)

	Bangladesh 2000	India 1999	Mali 2001	Uganda 1995	Zimbabwe 1994
Constant	-3.098**	-2.479**	-2.042**	-2.140**	-2.544**
	(0.099)	(0.028)	(0.053)	(0.104)	(0.167)
Age (mother)	-0.119*	-0.214**	-0.145**	-0.080*	-0.176
	(0.061)	(0.030)	(0.033)	(0.065)	(0.150)
Age^2 (mother)	0.178*	0.337**	0.231**	0.110	-0.337
	(0.104)	(0.032)	(0.052)	(0.107)	(0.248)
Sex of child (1=female)	-0.156	0.060	-0.107*	-0.077	-0.414*
	(0.104)	(0.046)	(0.059)	(0.107)	(0.219)
Immediate breastfeeding (=1)	-0.413**	-0.473**	-0.176**	-0.040	-0.499*
	(0.121)	(0.062)	(0.062)	(0.110)	(0.219)
Complete vaccination (=1)	-2.396**	-2.453**	-1.961**	-1.928**	-3.454**
	(0.219)	(0.066)	(0.126)	(0.187)	(0.344)
First born (=1)	0.273	-0.076	-0.116	0.134	-0.317
	(0.185)	(0.081)	(0.114)	(0.195)	(0.382)
Preceding birth interval	-0.006*	-0.007**	-0.015**	-0.003*	0.012*
	(0.003)	(0.001)	(0.002)	(0.004)	(0.005)
Household size (IV)	0.181**	0.068**	0.014**	0.064*	0.035
	(0.049)	(0.016)	(0.004)	(0.042)	(0.073)
Female headed household (=1)	0.028	0.037	-0.107	-0.088	-0.002
	(0.254)	(0.097)	(0.108)	(0.142)	(0.235)
Asset index	-0.132	-0.086**	-0.066	-0.160	-0.013
	(0.111)	(0.026)	(0.042)	(0.103)	(0.128)
BMI of mother	-0.039*	0.048**	0.026*	-0.041*	-0.003
	(0.024)	(0.010)	(0.012)	(0.022)	(0.037)
BMI^2/100 of mother	0.469	0.459	-0.253	0.265	-0.370
	(0.271)	(0.120)	(0.155)	(0.310)	(0.366)
Mother has sec. education (=1)	-0.180	-0.210*	-0.305**	-0.507	0.053
	(0.160)	(0.063)	(0.218)	(0.306)	(0.293)
Health facility index	-0.630**	-0.301**	-0.384**	-0.284**	-0.394**
	(0.088)	(0.028)	(0.046)	(0.084)	(0.135)
Community characteristics					
Distance to health facility***	-0.003*	0.001	0.000	-0.018	-0.033
	(0.001)	(0.002)	(0.000)	(0.049)	(0.095)
Secondary education (%)	-0.587	-0.614*	-0.319	-0.006	-1.525*
	(0.418)	(0.204)	(0.463)	(0.431)	(0.595)
Children had fever (%)	0.753*	-0.297	0.062	0.479*	0.333
	(0.418)	(0.255)	(0.181)	(0.252)	(0.480)
Public infrastruct. index	0.041*	-0.014	0.003	0.129*	0.261*
	(0.065)	(0.025)	(0.039)	(0.067)	(0.127)
Pseudo R^2	0.099	0.128	0.068	0.068	0.159
Obs.	5381	28539	9852	4232	1568

Source: Demographic and Health Surveys (DHS); own calculations.
Notes: *P-value<0.1. **P-value<0.01. For details about the variables, see Section 3.3.1. ***In the case of Bangladesh distance is measured in time (hours). The household size enters via an instrumental variable into the model. As instrument the mean household size per cluster is used.

Table A.3: Regression Results of Stunting (Logistic Regression)
(Old Reference Standard)

	Bangladesh 2000	India 1999	Mali 2001	Uganda 1995	Zimbabwe 1994
Constant	-0.594**	-0.301**	-0.619**	-0.749**	-1.144**
	(0.046)	(0.014)	(0.035)	(0.168)	(0.097)
Age (child)	0.105**	0.235**	0.146**	0.165**	0.304**
	(0.007)	(0.005)	(0.006)	(0.012)	(0.031)
Age^2 (child)	-0.001**	-0.006**	0.002**	-0.003**	-0.006**
	(0.000)	(0.000)	(0.000)	(0.000)	(0.001)
Sex of child (1=female)	0.029	0.008	-0.055	-0.235**	-0.051
	(0.060)	(0.024)	(0.046)	(0.067)	(0.114)
Immediate breastfeeding (=1)	-0.110*	-0.070*	-0.123*	-0.053*	-0.063
	(0.097)	(0.028)	(0.048)	(0.115)	(0.115)
Complete vaccination (=1)	-0.371*	-0.101*	0.134	-0.051	0.168
	(0.136)	(0.421)	(0.100)	(0.068)	(0.293)
First born (=1)	-0.248*	-0.293**	-0.300**	-0.193*	-0.244
	(0.097)	(0.389)	(0.083)	(0.115)	(0.193)
Preceding birth interval	-0.008**	-0.005**	-0.009**	-0.008	-0.004
	(0.001)	(0.001)	(0.001)	(0.002)	(0.003)
Household size (IV)	0.038	0.069*	-0.005	-0.034	0.056
	(0.026)	(0.009)	(0.003)	(0.024)	(0.037)
Female headed household (=1)	-0.143	-0.141**	-0.102	0.036	-0.122
	(0.133)	(0.050)	(0.082)	(0.086)	(0.123)
Asset index	-0.430**	-0.172**	-0.085**	-0.213**	-0.195**
	(0.061)	(0.013)	(0.033)	(0.064)	(0.071)
BMI of mother	-0.091**	-0.066**	-0.074**	-0.070**	-0.060**
	(0.014)	(0.005)	(0.009)	(0.014)	(0.019)
BMI^2/100 of mother	0.332	-0.091	-0.253	-0.117	0.241
	(0.212)	(0.081)	(0.155)	(0.252)	(0.248)
Mother has sec. education (=1)	-0.344**	-0.229**	-0.483**	0.281*	-0.351*
	(0.085)	(0.030)	(0.156)	(0.114)	(0.155)
Health facility index	-0.249**	-0.252**	-0.070**	-0.065**	-0.238**
	(0.047)	(0.015)	(0.032)	(0.056)	(0.084)
Community characteristics					
Distance to health facility***	0.001	-0.001	0.000	0.037	0.043
	(0.001)	(0.001)	(0.002)	(0.003)	(0.052)
Secondary education (%)	-0.167	-1.244**	-2.400**	-1.302**	-0.176
	(0.226)	(0.100)	(0.375)	(0.265)	(0.324)
Children had fever (%)	0.253	-0.602**	0.114	-0.454**	-0.260
	(0.186)	(0.121)	(0.143)	(0.155)	(0.253)
Public infrastruct. index	0.056	-0.007	-0.092**	-0.067	-0.025
	(0.036)	(0.012)	(0.030)	(0.045)	(0.077)
Pseudo R^2	0.109	0.140	0.118	0.108	0.121
Obs.	5284	34797	9258	4518	2057

Source: Demographic and Health Surveys (DHS); own calculations.
Notes: *P-value<0.1. **P-value<0.01. For details about the variables, see Section 3.3.1. ***In the case of Bangladesh distance is measured in time (hours). The household size enters via an instrumental variable into the model. As instrument the mean household size per cluster is used.

Table A.4: Regression Results of Stunting (Logistic Regression)
(New Reference Standard)

	Bangladesh 2000	India 1999	Mali 2001	Uganda 1995	Zimbabwe 1994
Constant	-0.245**	-0.093**	-0.327**	-0.344**	-0.885**
	(0.090)	(0.013)	(0.033)	(0.063)	(0.082)
Age (child)	0.104**	0.142**	0.125**	0.125**	0.172**
	(0.007)	(0.005)	(0.005)	(0.010)	(0.023)
Age^2 (child)	-0.001**	-0.002**	-0.002**	-0.002**	-0.003**
	(0.000)	(0.000)	(0.000)	(0.000)	(0.001)
Sex of child (1=female)	-0.059	-0.125**	-0.136**	-0.337**	-0.196*
	(0.058)	(0.022)	(0.044)	(0.063)	(0.101)
Immediate breastfeeding (=1)	-0.113*	-0.084**	-0.128*	-0.092**	-0.298*
	(0.061)	(0.026)	(0.045)	(0.064)	(0.171)
Complete vaccination (=1)	0.102	0.025	0.226	0.007	0.145
	(0.127)	(0.037)	(0.088)	(0.145)	(0.237)
First born (=1)	-0.168*	-0.219**	-0.167**	-0.171	-0.298*
	(0.094)	(0.036)	(0.078)	(0.107)	(0.171)
Preceding birth interval	-0.007**	-0.004**	-0.007**	-0.007	-0.005
	(0.001)	(0.001)	(0.001)	(0.002)	(0.003)
Household size (IV)	0.021	0.059**	-0.008**	-0.034	0.032
	(0.025)	(0.008)	(0.003)	(0.022)	(0.033)
Female headed household (=1)	-0.084	-0.103*	-0.171*	-0.091	-0.125
	(0.128)	(0.046)	(0.078)	(0.081)	(0.110)
Asset index	-0.388**	-0.159**	-0.114**	-0.227**	-0.150**
	(0.058)	(0.012)	(0.031)	(0.060)	(0.062)
BMI of mother	-0.073**	-0.056**	-0.059**	-0.061**	-0.048**
	(0.014)	(0.012)	(0.008)	(0.013)	(0.018)
$BMI^2/100$ of mother	0.379*	-0.075	-0.165	-0.405*	0.126
	(0.150)	(0.070)	(0.121)	(0.238)	(0.208)
Mother has sec. education (=1)	-0.285**	-0.199**	-0.412**	-0.159	-0.249*
	(0.080)	(0.028)	(0.137)	(0.105)	(0.135)
Health facility index	-0.216**	-0.231**	-0.087*	-0.099*	-0.172*
	(0.044)	(0.014)	(0.030)	(0.051)	(0.077)
Community characteristics					
Distance to health facility***	0.001	-0.004*	0.000	0.029	0.017
	(0.001)	(0.001)	(0.000)	(0.028)	(0.047)
Secondary education (%)	-0.246**	-1.118**	-1.850**	-1.122**	-0.304
	(0.218)	(0.093)	(0.330)	(0.244)	(0.287)
Children had fever (%)	0.294	-0.586**	0.120	-0.514**	-0.189
	(0.181)	(0.113)	(0.136)	(0.146)	(0.236)
Public infrastruct. index	-0.001*	-0.001	-0.062**	-0.120**	-0.049
	(0.034)	(0.012)	(0.028)	(0.042)	(0.068)
Pseudo R^2	0.100	0.114	0.100	0.094	0.097
Obs.	5503	37880	9750	4771	2114

Source: Demographic and Health Surveys (DHS); own calculations.
Notes: *P-value<0.1. **P-value<0.01. For details about the variables, see Section 3.3.1. ***In the case of Bangladesh distance is measured in time (hours). The household size enters via an instrumental variable into the model. As instrument the mean household size per cluster is used.

Table A.5: Regression Results of Stunting (OLS Regression)
(Old Reference Standard)

	Bangladesh 2000	India 1999	Mali 2001	Uganda 1995	Zimbabwe 1994
Constant	-1.643**	-1.769**	-1.482**	-1.421**	-1.065**
	(0.024)	(0.009)	(0.024)	(0.040)	(0.042)
Age (child)	-0.065**	-0.167**	-0.110**	-0.111**	-0.139**
	(0.004)	(0.003)	(0.004)	(0.006)	(0.010)
Age^2 (child)	0.001**	0.003**	0.001**	0.002**	0.003**
	(0.000)	(0.000)	(0.000)	(0.000)	(0.000)
Sex of child (1=female)	-0.037	-0.004	0.077**	0.189**	0.073
	(0.034)	(0.016)	(0.033)	(0.041)	(0.053)
Immediate breastfeeding (=1)	0.104**	0.089**	0.089**	0.102*	-0.041
	(0.035)	(0.019)	(0.034)	(0.042)	(0.054)
Complete vaccination (=1)	0.334	0.112	0.134*	0.124	0.202*
	(0.354)	(0.027)	(0.625)	(0.072)	(0.199)
First born (=1)	0.152**	0.207**	0.228**	0.115**	0.174*
	(0.054)	(0.026)	(0.059)	(0.068)	(0.088)
Preceding birth interval	0.005**	0.004**	0.007**	0.007**	0.004
	(0.001)	(0.000)	(0.000)	(0.001)	(0.001)
Household size (IV)	-0.028**	-0.056**	0.004*	0.038*	-0.017
	(0.015)	(0.006)	(0.002)	(0.015)	(0.018)
Female headed household (=1)	0.088	0.025	0.039	-0.007	0.011
	(0.074)	(0.033)	(0.059)	(0.052)	(0.058)
Asset index	0.240**	0.121**	0.056**	0.189**	0.145**
	(0.033)	(0.008)	(0.023)	(0.037)	(0.032)
BMI of mother	0.070**	0.060**	0.065**	0.051**	0.042**
	(0.008)	(0.003)	(0.006)	(0.009)	(0.009)
BMI^2/100 of mother	-0.252*	-0.052	0.020	0.159	-0.107
	(0.110)	(0.046)	(0.076)	(0.127)	(0.103)
Mother has sec. education (=1)	0.188**	0.127**	0.402**	0.118*	0.162*
	(0.046)	(0.020)	(0.090)	(0.065)	(0.070)
Health facility index	0.146**	0.187**	0.047*	0.010	0.064
	(0.026)	(0.010)	(0.023)	(0.034)	(0.042)
Community characteristics					
Distance to health facility***	0.000	0.002**	0.000	-0.046*	0.002
	(0.000)	(0.001)	(0.000)	(0.019)	(0.026)
Secondary education (%)	0.276*	0.850**	1.256**	0.596**	0.313*
	(0.127)	(0.066)	(0.214)	(0.151)	(0.151)
Children had fever (%)	-0.221*	0.380**	-0.178*	0.221*	0.085
	(0.105)	(0.081)	(0.103)	(0.095)	(0.123)
Public infrastruct. index	-0.011	0.008	0.059**	0.030	0.021
	(0.020)	(0.008)	(0.021)	(0.026)	(0.035)
R^2	0.184	0.214	0.174	0.161	0.193
Obs.	5284	34797	9258	4518	2057

Source: Demographic and Health Surveys (DHS); own calculations.
Notes: *P-value<0.1. **P-value<0.01. For details about the variables, see Section 3.3.1. ***In the case of Bangladesh distance is measured in time (hours). The household size enters via an instrumental variable into the model. As instrument the mean household size per cluster is used.

Table A.6: Regression Results of Stunting Z-Scores (OLS Regression) (New Reference Standard)

	Bangladesh 2000	India 1999	Mali 2001	Uganda 1995	Zimbabwe 1994
Constant	-1.925**	-2.152**	-1.610**	-1.826**	-1.253**
	(0.120)	(0.018)	(0.062)	(0.069)	(0.063)
Age (child)	-0.068**	-0.152**	-0.136**	-0.127**	-0.157**
	(0.019)	(0.006)	(0.009)	(0.010)	(0.015)
Age^2 (child)	0.001*	0.002**	0.002**	0.002**	0.003**
	(0.000)	(0.000)	(0.000)	(0.000)	(0.000)
Sex of child (1=female)	-0.230	0.177**	0.001	0.217**	0.194*
	(0.171)	(0.032)	(0.085)	(0.071)	(0.079)
Immediate breastfeeding (=1)	0.020*	0.059	0.084	0.266**	-0.009
	(0.180)	(0.038)	(0.088)	(0.073)	(0.080)
Complete vaccination (=1)	0.285	-0.008	0.056	0.272	0.267*
	(0.375)	(0.544)	(0.160)	(0.126)	(0.159)
First born (=1)	0.188	0.138**	0.332*	-0.115	0.244*
	(0.276)	(0.052)	(0.151)	(0.119)	(0.130)
Preceding birth interval	0.010	0.004**	0.008	0.006*	0.005
	(0.004)	(0.001)	(0.003)	(0.002)	(0.002)
Household size (IV)	0.037	-0.085**	0.002	0.033	0.010
	(0.074)	(0.011)	(0.005)	(0.025)	(0.027)
Female headed household (=1)	1.170**	0.025	-0.013	0.106	0.077
	(0.380)	(0.066)	(0.151)	(0.091)	(0.085)
Asset index	0.056	0.159**	0.127**	0.187**	0.131**
	(0.167)	(0.017)	(0.059)	(0.065)	(0.047)
BMI of mother	0.097*	0.047**	0.070**	0.028**	0.039**
	(0.040)	(0.007)	(0.016)	(0.015)	(0.014)
BMI^2/100 of mother	-0.356	-0.091	0.196	0.201*	-0.167
	(0.449)	(0.091)	(0.196)	(0.201)	(0.149)
Mother has sec. education (=1)	0.112	0.170**	0.281	0.083	0.183*
	(0.233)	(0.040)	(0.235)	(0.115)	(0.102)
Health facility index	0.131	0.234**	0.042	0.049	0.070
	(0.132)	(0.020)	(0.058)	(0.059)	(0.060)
Community characteristics					
Distance to health facility***	-0.004*	0.006**	0.000	-0.004	0.021
	(0.002)	(0.002)	(0.000)	(0.033)	(0.038)
Secondary education (%)	0.071	0.944**	1.309*	0.684*	0.506*
	(0.643)	(0.132)	(0.550)	(0.265)	(0.222)
Children had fever (%)	0.362	0.319**	-0.369	0.286*	0.157
	(0.534)	(0.161)	(0.264)	(0.166)	(0.182)
Public infrastruct. index	0.002	0.014	0.020	0.096*	-0.024
	(0.101)	(0.016)	(0.053)	(0.046)	(0.051)
R^2	0.018	0.080	0.038	0.073	0.157
Obs.	5517	37943	9755	3383	2117

Source: Demographic and Health Surveys (DHS); own calculations.

Notes: *P-value<0.1. **P-value<0.01. For details about the variables, see Section 3.3.1. ***In the case of Bangladesh distance is measured in time (hours). The household size enters via an instrumental variable into the model. As instrument the mean household size per cluster is used.

Table A.7: Regression Results of Stunting Z-Scores (Multilevel Regression)
(New Reference Standard)

	Bangladesh 2000	India 1999	Mali 2001	Uganda 1995	Zimbabwe 1994
Constant	-0.702**	-0.155**	0.720**	-0.162**	0.229**
	(0.051)	(0.030)	(0.045)	(0.071)	(0.083)
Age (child)	-0.065**	-0.169**	-0.114**	-0.108**	-0.142**
	(0.004)	(0.003)	(0.004)	(0.006)	(0.010)
Age^2 (child)	0.001**	0.003**	0.002**	0.002**	0.003**
	(0.000)	(0.000)	(0.000)	(0.000)	(0.000)
Sex of child (1=female)	0.034	0.003	0.091**	0.188**	0.069
	(0.171)	(0.032)	(0.085)	(0.071)	(0.079)
Immediate breastfeeding (=1)	0.109**	0.032	0.063	0.100*	-0.035
	(0.036)	(0.020)	(0.035)	(0.042)	(0.054)
Complete vaccination (=1)	0.358	-0.002	-0.095	0.124	-0.205*
	(0.746)	(0.027)	(0.061)	(0.072)	(0.109)
First born (=1)	0.146**	0.203**	0.241**	0.120	0.177*
	(0.054)	(0.026)	(0.058)	(0.068)	(0.088)
Preceding birth interval	0.005**	0.004**	0.008**	0.007**	0.004**
	(0.001)	(0.000)	(0.001)	(0.001)	(0.001)
Household size (IV)	-0.023	-0.043**	0.003	0.046**	-0.017
	(0.017)	(0.011)	(0.004)	(0.017)	(0.019)
Female headed household (=1)	0.098	0.036	-0.009	-0.022	0.004
	(0.075)	(0.032)	(0.059)	(0.052)	(0.058)
Asset index	0.232**	0.117**	0.059*	0.166**	0.119**
	(0.034)	(0.008)	(0.026)	(0.040)	(0.033)
BMI of mother	0.068**	0.057**	0.059**	0.051**	0.041**
	(0.008)	(0.003)	(0.006)	(0.009)	(0.009)
BMI^2/100 of mother	-0.250*	0.048	0.027	0.154	-0.110
	(0.110)	(0.058)	(0.074)	(0.130)	(0.103)
Mother has sec. education (=1)	0.193**	0.136**	0.123**	0.123*	0.160*
	(0.046)	(0.020)	(0.087)	(0.064)	(0.069)
Health facility index	0.139**	0.176**	-0.004	0.018	0.063
	(0.026)	(0.011)	(0.024)	(0.036)	(0.040)
Community characteristics					
Distance to health facility***	0.000	0.004	-0.002	-0.005*	0.001
	(0.001)	(0.002)	(0.003)	(0.002)	(0.002)
Secondary education (%)	0.277*	0.935**	1.744**	0.622**	0.321*
	(0.149)	(0.138)	(0.303)	(0.172)	(0.158)
Children had fever (%)	-0.208*	0.329*	-0.236	0.181	0.078*
	(0.126)	(0.183)	(0.169)	(0.116)	(0.131)
Public infrastruct. index	-0.011	0.019	0.054*	0.030	0.016
	(0.024)	(0.016)	(0.033)	(0.032)	(0.036)
R^2	0.184	0.214	0.174	0.160	0.191
Obs. (level 1)	5284	34797	9258	4518	2057
Obs. (level 2)	339	424	368	359	229

Source: Demographic and Health Surveys (DHS); own calculations.
Notes:*P-value<0.1. **P-value<0.01. For details about the variables, see Section 3.3.1. ***In the case of Bangladesh distance is measured in time (hours). The household size enters via an instrumental variable into the model. As instrument the mean household size per cluster is used.

Table A.8: Regression Results of Stunting Z-Scores (Multilevel Regression) (New Reference Standard)

	Bangladesh 2000	India 1999	Mali 2001	Uganda 1995	Zimbabwe 1994
Constant	-0.807**	-0.459**	-1.600**	-0.288**	0.362**
	(0.246)	(0.057)	(0.071)	(0.121)	(0.121)
Age (child)	-0.069**	-0.155**	-0.139**	-0.126**	-0.157**
	(0.019)	(0.006)	(0.010)	(0.010)	(0.015)
Age^2 (child)	0.001*	0.002**	0.002**	0.002**	0.003**
	(0.000)	(0.000)	(0.000)	(0.000)	(0.000)
Sex of child (1=female)	-0.230	0.178**	0.005	0.213	0.193*
	(0.171)	(0.032)	(0.085)	(0.071)	(0.079)
Immediate breastfeeding (=1)	0.008	0.056	0.089	0.262**	0.002
	(0.180)	(0.039)	(0.090)	(0.073)	(0.080)
Complete vaccination (=1)	0.280	-0.025	0.863	0.277	0.279*
	(0.375)	(0.054)	(0.159)	(0.123)	(0.159)
First born (=1)	0.191	0.135**	0.340*	-0.110	0.239
	(0.276)	(0.052)	(0.151)	(0.119)	(0.130)
Preceding birth interval	0.010*	0.005**	0.009**	0.006**	0.005
	(0.004)	(0.001)	(0.003)	(0.002)	(0.002)
Household size (IV)	0.039	-0.085**	0.003	0.028	0.011
	(0.075)	(0.019)	(0.007)	(0.028)	(0.028)
Female headed household (=1)	1.170	0.012**	-0.049	0.084	0.076
	(0.380)	(0.066)	(0.154)	(0.092)	(0.085)
Asset index	0.157**	0.151**	0.131**	0.166*	0.132**
	(0.067)	(0.017)	(0.063)	(0.068)	(0.049)
BMI of mother	0.097*	0.049**	0.068**	0.029*	0.038*
	(0.040)	(0.007)	(0.017)	(0.015)	(0.014)
BMI^2/100 of mother	-0.354	-0.147	0.008	0.379*	-0.167
	(0.446)	(0.091)	(0.196)	(0.201)	(0.149)
Mother has sec. education (=1)	0.110	0.184**	0.278	0.094	0.185*
	(0.133)	(0.040)	(0.233)	(0.114)	(0.102)
Health facility index	0.130	0.221**	0.043	0.038	0.098
	(0.132)	(0.021)	(0.061)	(0.062)	(0.062)
Community characteristics					
Distance to health facility***	-0.004*	0.008*	0.000	-0.005	0.000
	(0.002)	(0.004)	(0.005)	(0.004)	(0.002)
Secondary education (%)	0.068	0.840**	1.289*	0.644*	0.467*
	(0.651)	(0.246)	(0.641)	(0.288)	(0.233)
Children had fever (%)	0.364	0.234	-0.379	0.259	0.153
	(0.541)	(0.324)	(0.326)	(0.190)	(0.193)
Public infrastruct. index	0.002	0.045	0.015	0.082	-0.028
	(0.102)	(0.030)	(0.064)	(0.052)	(0.054)
R^2	0.018	0.080	0.040	0.080	0.156
Obs. (level 1)	5517	37943	9755	4777	2117
Obs. (level 2)	339	424	368	359	229

Source: Demographic and Health Surveys (DHS); own calculations.
Notes:*P-value<0.1. **P-value<0.01. For details about the variables, see Section 3.3.1. ***In the case of Bangladesh distance is measured in time (hours). The household size enters via an instrumental variable into the model. As instrument the mean household size per cluster is used.

Appendix D

Table A.1: Data sources for developing countries

Country	Year	Type of survey
Burkina Faso	2003	Demographic and Health Survey (DHS)
	2003	Enquête Prioritaire sur les Conditions de Vie des Ménages EP)
Bolivia	2003	Demographic and Health Survey (DHS)
	2002	Living Standard Measurement Survey (LSMS)
Côte d'Ivoire	1999	Demographic and Health Survey (DHS)
	1998	Enquête de Niveau de Vie des Ménages (ENV)
Cameroon	2004	Demographic and Health Survey (DHS)
	2001	Enquête Camerounaise auprès des Ménages (ECAM)
Colombia	2005	Demographic and Health Survey (DHS)
	2003	Encuesta de Calidad de Vida
Guinea	1999	Demographic and Health Survey (DHS)
	1995	Enquête Intégrale avec Module Budget et Consummation
Indonesia	2003	Demographic and Health Survey (DHS)
	2000	Indonesian Family Life Survey (3rd wave) (IFLS)
Madagascar	1997	Demographic and Health Survey (DHS)
	2001	Enquête auprès des Ménages (EPM)
Mozambique	2003	Demographic and Health Survey (DHS)
	2002	Inquérito Nacional aos Agregados Familiares sobre as Condicões de Vida
Nicaragua	2001	Demographic and Health Survey (DHS)
	2001	Encuesta Nacional de Hogares sobre Medición de Nivel de Vida (EMNV)
South Africa	1998	Demographic and Health Survey (DHS)
	2000	Income and Expenditure Survey
Vietnam	2002	Demographic and Health Survey (DHS)
	2004	Living Standard Measurement Survey (LSMS)
Zambia	2002	Demographic and Health Survey (DHS)
	2002	Living Conditions Monitoring Survey (LCMS)

Table A.2: Quintile specific life expectancy indices by country

	$Q=1$	$Q=2$	$Q=3$	$Q=4$	$Q=5$	All	Ratio $Q5/Q1$
(a) L^Q computed using predicted income							
Industrialized Countries							
USA (2000)	0.82	0.86	0.88	0.89	0.90	0.87	1.098
Finland (2000)	0.85	0.87	0.89	0.91	0.93	0.89	1.094
Developing Countries							
Colombia (2003/2005)	0.814	0.781	0.801	0.799	0.788	0.797	0.968
Vietnam (2004/2002)	0.713	0.707	0.825	0.812	0.849	0.764	1.191
Indonesia (2000/2003)	0.650	0.651	0.711	0.711	0.799	0.697	1.229
South Africa (2000/1998)	0.416	0.468	0.532	0.542	0.523	0.481	1.257
Bolivia (2002/2003)	0.632	0.622	0.666	0.691	0.681	0.651	1.078
Nicaragua (2001/2001)	0.730	0.700	0.753	0.756	0.783	0.735	1.073
Cameroon (2001/2004)	0.370	0.335	0.337	0.323	0.342	0.344	0.924
Madagascar (2001/1997)	0.509	0.432	0.463	0.574	0.574	0.500	1.128
Guinea (1995/1999)	0.532	0.491	0.473	0.455	0.415	0.479	0.780
Côte d'Ivoire (1998/1999)	0.369	0.394	0.296	0.306	0.427	0.364	1.158
Zambia (2002/2002)	0.214	0.200	0.205	0.209	0.211	0.208	0.986
Mozambique (2002/2003)	0.329	0.309	0.263	0.226	0.219	0.281	0.666
Burkina Faso (2003/2003)	0.385	0.386	0.382	0.359	0.359	0.375	0.932
(b) L^Q computed using asset index							
Colombia (2003/2005)	0.787	0.791	0.831	0.870	0.777	0.797	0.987
Vietnam (2004/2002)	0.684	0.751	0.799	0.835	0.877	0.764	1.282
Indonesia (2000/2003)	0.616	0.631	0.679	0.764	0.890	0.697	1.445
South Africa (2000/1998)	0.405	0.476	0.530	0.504	0.602	0.481	1.486
Bolivia (2002/2003)	0.600	0.627	0.682	0.667	0.811	0.651	1.352
Nicaragua (2001/2001)	0.678	0.745	0.756	0.759	0.828	0.735	1.221
Cameroon (2001/2004)	0.328	0.328	0.365	0.330	0.391	0.344	1.192
Madagascar (2001/1997)	0.429	0.509	0.498	0.556	0.567	0.500	1.322
Guinea (1995/1999)	0.415	0.458	0.431	0.562	0.624	0.479	1.504
Côte d'Ivoire (1998/1999)	0.317	0.384	0.340	0.464	0.384	0.364	1.211
Zambia (2002/2002)	0.185	0.215	0.209	0.196	0.246	0.208	1.330
Mozambique (2002/2003)	0.264	0.276	0.277	0.310	0.312	0.281	1.182
Burkina Faso (2003/2003)	0.345	0.386	0.373	0.368	0.420	0.375	1.217

Note: For developing countries the years in brackets refer to the respective survey years. The first year refers to the HIS data set, the second to the DHS data set. All indices are rescaled to UNDP's reported HDI value of the second survey year.
Source: Household Income Survey (HIS) and Demographic and Health Surveys (DHS) (see Table A1), Human Development Reports; calculations by the authors.

Table A.3: Quintile specific education indices by country

	$Q=1$	$Q=2$	$Q=3$	$Q=4$	$Q=5$	All	Ratio $Q5/Q1$
Industrialized Country							
USA	0.94	0.96	0.98	0.99	1.02	0.98	1.085
Finland	0.97	0.97	0.98	0.99	1.02	0.99	1.052
Developing Country							
Colombia (2003/2005)	0.788	0.834	0.866	0.887	0.932	0.863	1.18
Vietnam (2004/2002)	0.783	0.807	0.821	0.867	0.880	0.831	1.12
Indonesia (2000/2003)	0.730	0.789	0.821	0.855	0.900	0.814	1.23
South Africa (2000/1998)	0.814	0.818	0.823	0.824	0.824	0.821	1.01
Bolivia (2002/2003)	0.721	0.833	0.888	0.922	0.954	0.870	1.32
Nicaragua (2001/2001)	0.621	0.635	0.666	0.688	0.722	0.665	1.16
Cameroon (2001/2004)	0.579	0.664	0.716	0.752	0.801	0.713	1.38
Madagascar (2001/1997)	0.462	0.598	0.612	0.648	0.822	0.593	1.78
Guinea (1995/1999)	0.304	0.433	0.442	0.486	0.462	0.410	1.52
Côte d'Ivoire (1998/1999)	0.367	0.417	0.448	0.490	0.546	0.443	1.49
Zambia (2002/2002)	0.586	0.657	0.707	0.771	0.831	0.704	1.42
Mozambique (2002/2003)	0.433	0.459	0.460	0.464	0.524	0.471	1.21
Burkina Faso (2003/2003)	0.194	0.207	0.228	0.259	0.373	0.260	1.92

Note: For developing countries the years in brackets refer to the respective survey years. The first year refers to the HIS data set, the second to the DHS data set. All indices are rescaled to UNDP's reported HDI value of the second survey year.
Source: Household Income Survey (HIS) and Demographic and Health Surveys (DHS) (see Table A1), Human Development Reports; calculations by the authors.

Table A.4: Quintile specific GDP indices by country

	$Q = 1$	$Q = 2$	$Q = 3$	$Q = 4$	$Q = 5$	All	Ratio $Q5/Q1$
Industrialized Country							
USA	0.75	0.87	0.93	0.99	1.11	0.97	1.480
Finland	0.82	0.88	0.92	0.96	1.04	0.94	1.146
Developing Country							
Colombia (2003/2005)	0.444	0.598	0.702	0.815	1.072	0.711	2.41
Vietnam (2004/2002)	0.415	0.482	0.534	0.592	0.726	0.543	1.75
Indonesia (2000/2003)	0.433	0.533	0.599	0.673	0.832	0.593	1.92
South Africa (2000/1998)	0.462	0.624	0.748	0.901	1.211	0.773	2.62
Bolivia (2002/2003)	0.329	0.459	0.543	0.634	0.825	0.548	2.51
Nicaragua (2001/2001)	0.296	0.507	0.611	0.714	0.939	0.599	3.18
Cameroon (2001/2004)	0.345	0.439	0.505	0.576	0.738	0.513	2.14
Madagascar (2001/1997)	0.139	0.281	0.377	0.484	0.664	0.370	4.79
Guinea (1995/1999)	0.300	0.480	0.598	0.735	1.002	0.514	3.34
Côte d'Ivoire (1998/1999)	0.344	0.446	0.515	0.591	0.753	0.483	2.19
Zambia (2002/2002)	0.179	0.297	0.376	0.462	0.672	0.366	3.75
Mozambique (2002/2003)	0.218	0.329	0.401	0.477	0.676	0.409	3.10
Burkina Faso (2003/2003)	0.232	0.325	0.393	0.470	0.675	0.409	2.91

Note: For developing countries the years in brackets refer to the respective survey years. The first year refers to the HIS data set, the second to the DHS data set. All indices are rescaled to UNDP's reported HDI value of the second survey year. *Source:* Household Income Survey (HIS) and Demographic and Health Surveys (DHS) (see Table A1), Human Development Reports; calculations by the authors.

Bibliography

Adebayo, S., L. Fahrmeir and S. Klasen (2004), Analyzing Infant Mortality with Geoadditive Categorial Regression Models: A Case Study for Nigeria, *Economics and Human Biology*, 2: 229-244.

Adams, R.H. (2004), Economic Growth, Inequality and Poverty: Estimating the Growth Elasticity of Poverty. *World Development* 32(12): 1989-2014.

Ahmed, S.M., A. Adams, A.M.R. Chowdhuri, and A. Bhuiya (1998), Chronic Energy Deficiency in Women from Rural Bangladesh: Some Socioeconomic Determinants, *Journal of Biosocial Science*, 30: 349-358.

Anand S. and A. Sen (1992), Human Development Index: Methodology and Measurement, Human Development Report Office Occasional Paper 12, New York: UNDP.

Atkin, M, D. Anderson, and J. Hinde (1981), Statistical modelling of data on teaching styles (with discussion), *Journal of the Royal Statistical Society*, 144: 148-161.

Barker, M., G. Chorghade, S. Crozier, S. Leary, and C. Fall (2006), Gender Differences in Body Mass Index in Rural India are Determined by Socio-Economic Factors and Lifestyle, *The Journal of Nutrition*, 136: 3062-3068.

Behrman, J.R., Alderman H. and J. Hoddinott (2004), Malnutrition and Hunger, In: Lomborg (ed.), *Global Crises, Global Solutions*, Cambridge: Cambridge University Press, pp. 363-420.

Bennett, N. (1976), *Teaching Style and Pupil Progress*, London: Open Books.

Bhalla, S.S. (2003), Recounting the Poor: Poverty in India, 1983-1999, *Economic and Political Weekly* 37(4): 338-349.

Bhalla, S.S. (2002), *Imagine There is No Country: Poverty, Inequality and Growth in the Era of Globalization*, Washington: Institute for International Economics.

Bhalla, S.S. (2001). How to Over-Estimate Poverty: Detailed Examination of the NSS 1993 Data. *Paper presented for the 50th Anniversary of the National Sample Survey.*

Bhandari, N., Bahl, R., Taneja, S., de Onis, M. and M. Bhan (2002), Growth performance of affluent Indian children is similar to that in developed countries, *Bulletin of the WHO* 80(3): 189-195.

Bogin, B. (1988), *Patterns of Human Growth*, Cambridge: Cambridge University Press.

Bourguignon, F. (2003). The Growth Elasticity of Poverty Reduction: Explaining Heterogeneity across Countries and Time Periods. In T. Eichler and S. Turnovsky (eds.). *Growth and Inequality.* Cambridge: MIT Press.

Bryk, A.S. and S.W. Raudenbush (1992), *Hierarchical Linear Models: Applications and Data Analysis*, Newbury Park: Sage.

Coale A.J. and P. Demeny (1983), *Regional model life tables and stable populations.* 2. ed. New York/ London: Academic Press.

Cox, D.R. (1972), Regression Models and Life Tables (with Discussion), *Journal of the Royal Statistical Society*, Series B 34: 187-220.

Cutler D., A. Deaton and A. Lleras-Muney (2005), The Determinants of Mortality. *Journal of Economic Perspectives*, 20 (3): 97-120.

Datt, G. and M. Ravallion (2002), Is India's Economic Growth Leaving the Poor Behind?, *The Journal of Economic Perspectives* 16(3): 89-108.

Datt, G. and M. Ravallion (1992), Growth and Redistribution Components of Changes in Poverty Measures: A Decomposition with Application to Brazil and India in the 1980s. *Journal of Development Economics* 38(2): 275-295.

Davies, D.P. (1988), The importance of genetic influences on growth in early childhood with particular reference to children of asiatic origin, In: Waterlow, J. (ed.), *Linear Growth Retardation in Developing Countries*, New York: Raven.

Deaton A. (2005), Measuring Poverty in a Growing World (or Measuring Growth in a Poor World). *Review of Economics and Statistics*, 87(1): 1-19.

Deaton A. (2003a), Adjusted Indian Poverty Estimates for 1999-2000, *Economic and Political Weekly* 37(4): 322-326.

Deaton A. (2003b), Prices and Poverty in India: 1987-2000. *Economic and Political Weekly* 37(4): 362-368.

Deation A. and V. Kozel (2005), Data and Dogma: The Great Indian Poverty Debate. *The World Bank Research Observer*, 20(2): 177-199.

Deaton A. and S. Zaidi (2002), Guidelines for Constructing Consumption Aggregates for Welfare Analysis. Washington D.C.: World Bank.

Deaton, A. (1997), *The Analysis of Household Surveys. A Microeconomic Approach to Development Policy*, published for the World Bank, Baltimore and London: John Hopkins University Press.

de Onis, M. et al. for the WHO Multicentre Growth Reference Study Group (2004), The WHO Multicentre Growth Reference Study: planning, study design and methodology. *Food and Nutrition Bulletin* 25 (Suppl 1): S15-S26.

De Onis, M. and M. Blössner (2000), Prevalence and trends of overweight among preschool children in developing countries, *American Journal of Clinical Nutrition*, 72: 1032-1039.

de Onis, M. and J.P. Habicht (1996), Anthropometric reference data for international use: recommendations from a World Health Organization Expert Committee, *American Journal of Clinical Nutrition* 64: 650-658.

de Onis, M. and R. Yip (1996), The WHO growth chart: historical considerations and current scientific issues, *Bibliotheca Nutritio et Dieta* 53: 74-89.

Doak, C., L. Adair, C. Monteiro, and B. Popkin (2000), Overweight and underweight coexist within households in Brazil, China, and Russia, *Journal of Nutrition* 130 (12): 2965-2971.

Doak, C., L. Adair, M. Bentley, Z. Fendying, and B. Popkin (2002), The underweight/overweight household: An exploration of household sociodemographic and dietary factors in China, *Public Health Nutrition* 5 (1A): 215-221.

Eckhardt, C. L. (2006), Micronutrient Malnutrition, Obesity, and Chronic Disease in Countries Undergoing the Nutrition Transition: Potential Links and Program/Policy Implications, *IFPRI FCND Discussion Paper 213*.

Elbers C., J.O. Lanjouw and P. Lanjouw (2003), Micro-Level Estimation of Poverty and Inequality. *Econometrica*, 71 (1): 355-364.

Eliason, S.R. (1993), *Maximum Likelihood Estimation*, Newbury Park: Sage.

Engle, P., P. Menon, and C. Haddad (1999), Care and Nutrition: Concepts and Measurement, *World Development*, 27 (8): 1309-1337.

Eveleth, P.E. and J.M. Tanner (1990), *Worldwide Variations in Human Growth*, Cambridge: Cambridge University Press.

Filmer, D. and L.H. Pritchett (2001), Estimating Wealth Effects without Expenditure Data - or Tears: An Application to Educational Enrollments in States of India, *Demography*, 38 (1): 115-132.

Filmer D. and L. Pritchett (1999), The Effect of Household Wealth on Educational Attainment: Evidence from 35 countries. *Population and Development Review*, 25 (1): 85-120.

Foster J.E., L.F. López-Calva und M. Székely (2003), Measuring the Distribution of Human Development. Mimeo, Vanderbilt University, Nashiville.

Foster, J., Greer, J., and E. Thorbecke (1984), A class of decomposable poverty measures, *Econometrica*, 52: 761-5.

Garrett, J.L. and M.T. Ruel (2003), Stunted Child - Overweight Mother Pairs: An Emerging Policy Concern?, *IFPRI FCND Discussion Paper 148*.

Gillespie, S., J. Mason, and R. Martorell (1996), How Nutrition Improves, ACC / SCN Nutrition Policy Discussion Paper 15, United Nations Administrative Committee on Coordination / Sub-Committee on Nutrition, Geneva.

Goldstein, H. (1999), *Multilevel Statistical Models*, London: Arnold.

Goldstein, H. (1987), *Multilevel Models in Educational and Social Research*, London: Griffin.

Gopalan, C. (1992), Undernutrition: Measurement and Poverty, in S.R. Osmani (ed) *Undernutrition and Poverty*, Oxford: Oxford University Press.

Grosse, M., S. Klasen, and J. Spatz (2005), Creating National Poverty Profiles and Growth Incidence Curves with Incomplete Income or Consumption Expenditure Data, Background Paper for the Study: Operationalizing Pro-Poor Growth - Country Case Study Bolivia, Ibero-America Institute for Economic Research (IAI) Discussion Paper No. 129, University of Göttingen.

Grosse M., S. Klasen and J. Spatz (2005), Creating National Poverty Profiles and Growth Incidence Curves with Incomplete Income or Consumption Expenditure Data: An Application to Bolivia. Ibero America Institute for Econonomic Research (IAI) Discussion Papers No. 129, University of Göttingen.

Grün C. and S. Klasen (2006), Inequality, and Well-Being: Comparisons across space and time. Mimeo, University of Göttingen.

Haddad, L. and S. Gillespie (2001), Effective Food and Nutrition Policy Responses to HIV/AIDS: What We Know and Need to Know, FCND Discussion paper No. 112, International Food Policy Research Institute (IFPRI), Washington.

Hasin, A., R. Bequm, M.R. Khan, and F. Ahmed (1996), Relationship between birth weight and biochemical measures of maternal nutritional status at delivery in Bangladeshi urban poors, *International Journal of Food Sciences and Nutrition*, 43(3): 273-279.

Hox, J. (2002), *Multilevel Analysis - Techniques and Applications*, Mahwah: Erlbaum.

Kandala, N.B., S. Lang, L. Fahrmeir, and S. KLasen (2001), Semiparametric Analysis of the Socio-Demographic and Spatial Determinants of Chronic Undernutrition in Two African Countries, *Research in Official Statistics*, 4 (1): 81-100.

Kakwani, N. and E. Pernia (2000), What is Pro-Poor Growth?, *Asian Development Review*, 18 (1): 1-16.

Kakwani, Nanak (1993). Poverty and Economic Growth with Application to Côte d'Ivoire. *Review of Income and Wealth* 39(2): 121-139.

Kelley A.C. (1991), The Human Development Index: 'Handle with Care', *Population and Development Review*, 17 (2): 315-324.

Kim, S., Moon, S. and Popkin, B. M. (2000), The nutrition transition in South Korea, *American Journal of Clinical Nutrition* 71: 44-53.

Klasen, S. (2007), Poverty, undernutrition, and child mortality; some inter-regional puzzles and their implications for research and policy, *Journal of Economic Inequality*, forthcoming.

Klasen S. (2006a), Guest Editor's Introduction. *Journal of Human Development*, 7 (2): 145-159.

Klasen S. (2006b), UNDP´s Gender-Related Measures: Some Conceptual Problems and Possible Solutions. *Journal of Human Development*, 7 (2): 243-274.

Klasen, S. (2005), Economic Growth and Poverty Reduction: Measurement and Policy Issues, OECD Development Center Working Paper No. 246, OECD.

Klasen, S. (2004), In Search of the Holy Grail: How to Achieve Pro Poor Growth?, in Tungodden, B., N. Stern, and I. Kolstad (eds): *Toward Pro Poor Policies-Aid, Institutions, and Globalization*, New York: Oxford University Press.

Klasen, S. (2003), Malnourished and Surviving in South Asia, better Nourished and Dying Young in Africa: What can Explain this Puzzle? in FAO (eds) *Measurement and Assessment of Food Deprivation and Undernutrition*, Rome: FAO.

Klasen, S. (1996), Nutrition, Health, and Mortality in Sub-Saharan Africa: Is there a Gender Bias?, *Journal of Development Studies*, 32: 913-933.

Klasen, S. and A. Moradi (2000), The Nutritional Status of Elites in India, Kenya, and Zambia: An appropriate guide for developing reference standards for undernutrition?, Sonderforschungsbereich 386, University of Munich, Discussion Paper No. 217.

Ledermann S. (1969), *Nouvelles tables-types de mortalité*. Travaux et documents, Cahier n. 53, Paris: INED and PUF.

Maas, C.J.M. and J. Hox (2004), Robustness issues in multilevel regression analysis, *Statistica Neerlandica*, 58 (2): 127-137.

Marcoux, A. (2002), Sex Differentials in Undernutrition: A look at Survey Evidence, *Population and Development Review*, 28 (2): 275-284.

Martikainen P., P. Mäkelä, S. Koskinen and T. Valkonen (2001), Income differences in mortality: a register-based follow-up study of three million men and women. *International Journal of Epidemiology*, 30: 1397-1405.

Martorell, R., K.L. Kettel, M.L. Hughes, and L.M. Grummer-Strawn (1998), Obesity in Latin American women and children, *Journal of Nutrition*, 128: 1464-1473.

Mason, W.M., G.M. Wong, and B. Entwistle (1983), Contextual analysis through the multilevel linear model, *Sociological Methodology*, 13: 72-103.

Messer, E. (1986), The 'Small but Healthy' Hypothesis: Historical, Political and Ecological Influences on Nutritional Standards, *Human Ecology*, 14 (1): 57-75.

Michaelowa K. (2001), Primary Education Quality in Francophone Sub-Saharan Africa. *World Development*, 29 (10): 1699-1716.

Monteiro, C., W. Conde, and B. Popkin (2002), Is obesity replacing or adding to undernutrition? Evidence from different social classes in Brazil, *Public Health Nutrition* 5 (1A): 105-112.

Monteiro, C. A., Mondini, L., Medeiros de Souza, A. L., and Popkin, B. M. (1995), The nutrition transition in Brazil, *European Journal of Clinical Nutrition* 49: 105-113.

Monteiro, C., L. Mondini, A. Torres, and I. dos Reis (1997), Patterns of intra-familiar distribution of undernutrition: Methods and applications for developing societies, *European Journal of Clinical Nutrition* 51 (12): 800-803.

Morris, S. (2001), Measuring nutritional dimensions of household food security, In: J. Hoddinott (ed.), *Methods for rural development projects*, Washington D.C.: IFPRI.

Mosley, W.H. and L.C. Chen (1984), An Analytical Framework for the Study of Child Survival in Developing Countries, *Population and Development Review*, 10: 25-45.

Naiken (2003), FAO methodology for estimating the prevalence of food deprivation and undernutrition, In: FAO(ed) Measurement and Assessment of Food Deprivation and Undernutrition, Rome: FAO, pp.7-42.

Nandy, S., Irving, M., Gordon, D., Subramanian, S.V. and Smith, G.D. (2005), Poverty, child undernutrition and morbidity: new evidence from India, *Bulletin of the World Health Organization* 83 (3): 210-216.

Osmani, S.R. (1997), Poverty and Nutrition in South Asia, in *Nutrition and Poverty: papers from the ACC/SCN 24th Session Symposium*, Kathmandu, March 1997, United Nations Administrative Committee on Coordination, Sub-Committee on Nutrition.

Osberg, L. (2000), Schooling, Literacy and Individual Earnings, Statistics Canada, Ottawa, Canada.

Pebley, A.R., N. Goldman, and G. Rodriguez (1996), Prenatal and delivery care and Childhood immunization in Guatemala: do family and community matter?, *Demography*, 33: 231-247.

Pelletier, D.L. and E.A. Frongillo (2002), Changes in Child Survival are strongly Associated with Changes in Malnutrition in Developing Countries, *The Journal of Nutrition*, 133: 107-119.

Pelletier, D.L., E.A. Frongillo, Jr., D.G. Schroeder, and J.P. Habicht (1995), The effects of malnutrition on child mortality in developing countries, *Bulletin of the World Health Organization*, 73 (4): 443-448.

Pelletier, D. (1994), The relationship between child anthropometry and mortality in developing countries, *Journal of Nutrition*, (Supplement) 124: 2047S-2081S.

Popkin, B. M. (2001), The Nutrition Transition and Obesity in the Developing World, *The Journal of Nutrition* 131(3):871-873.

Popkin, B. M. (1998), The nutrition transition and its health implications in lower income countries, *Public Health Nutrition* 1: 5-21.

Popkin, B. M. (1994), The nutrition transition in low-income countries: an emerging crisis, *Nutrition Review* 52: 285-298.

Pritchett, L. and L.H. Summers (1996), Wealthier is healthier, *Journal of Human Ressources*, 31 (4): 841-868.

Ramalingaswami, V., U. Johsnon, and J. Rohde (1996), The Asian enigma, in *Progress of Nations*, New York: United Nations Childrens' Fund.

Ranis G., F. Stewart and E. Samman (2006), Human Development: beyond the HDI. QEH Working Paper Series - QEHWPS135.

Rao, S., C.S. Yajuik, A. Kanade, C.H.D. Fall, B.M. Margetts, A.A. Jackson, R. Shier, S. Joshi, S. Rege, H. Lubree, and B. Desai (2001), Intake of Micronutrient-Rich Foods in Rural Indian Mothers is Associated with the Size of their Babies at Birth: Pune Maternal Nutrition Study, *Journal of Nutrition*, 131: 1217-1224.

Ravallion M. (2001), Should Poverty Measures be Anchored to the National Accounts? *Economic and Political Weekly*, August 26-September 2: 3245-3252.

Ravallion M. (1997), Good and bad growth: The Human Development Reports. *World Development*, 25 (5): 631-638.

Ravallion, M. and S. Chen (1997). What can new survey data tell us about recent changes in distribution and poverty. *The World Bank Economic Review* 11: 357-382.

Ravallion, M. and M. Huppi (1991). Measuring changes in poverty: A methodological case study of Indonesia during an adjustment period. *The World Bank Economic Review* 5: 57-82.

Ray, D. (1998), *Development Economics*, Princeton: Princeton University Press.

Rogot E., P.D. Sorlie and N.J. Johnson (1992), Life Expectancy by Employment Status, Income, and Education in the National Longitudinal Mortality Study. *Public Health Reports*, 107 (4): 457-481.

Sagar A.D. and A. Najam (1998), The Human Development Index: A Critical Review. *Ecological Economics*, 25: 249-264.

Sahn, D.E. and D. Stiefel (2003), Exploring Alternative Measures of Welfare in the Absense of Expenditure Data, *Review of Income and Wealth*, 49 (4): 463-489.

Sahn D.E. and D.C. Stifel (2000), Poverty Comparisons Over Time and Across Countries in Africa. *World Development*, 28 (12): 2123-2155.

Seckler, D. (1982), Small but healthy: a basic hypothesis in the theory, measurement and policy of malnutrition, in: D. Sukhatme (ed) *Newer Concepts in Nutrition and their Implication for Policy*, Maharashtra Association for the Cultivation of Science, Pune.

Sen, A.K. (1988), The Concept of Development, in H. Chenery and T. Srinivasan (eds) *Handbook of Development Economics*, Vol. 1, 9-26.

Smith, L.C. and L. Haddad (2000), Explaining Child Malnutrition in Developing Countries, International Food Policy Research Institute (IFPRI), Washington.

Srinivasan T.N. (1994), Human Development: A New Paradigm or Reinvention of the Wheel? *American Economic Review*, 84 (2): 238-243.

Ssewanyana, S. and S. Younger (2004), Infant Mortality in Uganda: Determinants, Trends, and the Millennium Development Goals, Development Policy Research Unit (DPRU), University of Cape Town, South Africa.

Steenbergen, M.R. and B.S. Jones (2002), Modelling Multilevel Data Structures, *American Journal of Political Science*, 46 (1): 218-237.

Subbaro, K. and L. Rany (1995), Social gains from female education: A cross-national study, *Economic development and cultural change*, 44 (1): 105-128.

Svedberg, P. (2006), Declining child malnutrition: a reassessment, *International Journal of Epidemiology*, 35: 1336-1346.

Svedberg, P. (2002), Hunger in India - Facts and Challenges, Institute for International Economic Studies Seminar Paper No. 699, Stockholm.

Svedberg, P. (2002), Undernutrition Overestimated, *Economics of Cultural Change and Development*, 51(1): 5-36.

Svedberg, P. (2000), *Poverty and Undernutrition: Theory, Measurement and Policy*, Oxford: Oxford University Press.

Svedberg, P. (1999), 841 Million Undernourished? On the Tyranny of Deriving a Number, *World Development*, 27 (12): 2081-2098.

UN (2006), *The Human Development Report 2006*, New York: United Nations.

UN (2005), *The Millennium Development Goals Report 2005*, New York: United Nations.

UNDP (2006), *Human Development Report 2006. Beyond Scarcity: Power, Poverty and the Global Water Crisis*. UNDP, New York.

UNDP (2005), *Human Development Report 2005. International cooperation at a crossroads*. UNDP, New York.

UNDP (2000), Human Development Report 2000 Technical Report, pp. 269-273, New York, United Nations.

UNICEF (2004), Progress for Children - A Child Survival Report Card Vol 1, New York, UNICEF.

UNICEF (1998), The State of the Worlds' Children 1998, New York, UNICEF.

UNICEF (1990), Strategy for improved nutrition of children and women in developing countries, New York, UNICEF.

WHO (2006), *WHO Child Growth Standards - Length/ height-for-age, weight-for-age, weight-for-length and body mass index for age - Methods and Development*, Geneva: WHO.

WHO (2005), *Health and the Millennium Development Goals*, Geneva: WHO.

WHO (2004), *Global strategy on diet, physical activity, and health, Geneva: World Health Organization*, Geneva: WHO.

WHO (2002), *World Health Report 2001*, Geneva: World Health Organization.

WHO (1995), Physical Status: The Use and Interpretation of Anthropometry, WHO Technical Report Series No. 854, Geneva, World Health Organization.

WHO Multicentre Growth Reference Study Group (2006), WHO Child Growth Standards based on length/height, weight and age, *Acta Pediatrica*, Suppl. 450: 76-85.

WHO Working Group on Infant Growth (1994), An evaluation of infant growth, Geneva: World Health Organization.

World Bank (2007), Global Economic Prospects 2007 - Managing the next wave of globalization, Washington D.C.: The World Bank.

World Bank (2006), World Development Indicators 2006, CD-ROM. Washington: The World Bank.

World Bank (2005), World Development Indicators 2005, CD-ROM. Washington: The World Bank.

World Bank (1991). Growth, Poverty Alleviation and Improved Income Distribution in Malaysia: Changing Focus of Government Policy Intervention. Report 8667-MA. Washington: World Bank.

Göttinger Studien zur Entwicklungsökonomik
Göttingen Studies in Development Economics

Herausgegeben von/Edited by Hermann Sautter
und/and Stephan Klasen

Die Bände 1-8 sind über die Vervuert Verlagsgesellschaft (Frankfurt/M.) zu beziehen.

Bd./Vol. 9   Hermann Sautter / Rolf Schinke (eds.): Social Justice in a Market Economy. 2001.

Bd./Vol.10   Philipp Albert Theodor Kircher: Poverty Reduction Strategies. A comparative study applied to empirical research. 2002.

Bd./Vol.11   Matthias Blum: Weltmarktintegration, Wachstum und Innovationsverhalten in Schwellen ländern. Eine theoretische Diskussion mit einer Fallstudie über «Argentinien 1990-1999". 2003.

Bd./Vol.12   Jan Müller-Scheeßel: Die Privatisierung und Regulierung des Wassersektors. Das Beispiel Buenos Aires/Argentinien. 2003.

Bd./Vol.13   Ludger J. Löning: Economic Growth, Biodiversity Conservation, and the Formation of Human Capital in a Developing Country. 2004.

Bd./Vol.14   Silke Woltermann: Transitions in Segmented Labor Markets. The Case of Brazil. 2004.

Bd./Vol.15   Jörg Stosberg: Political Risk and the Institutional Environment for Foreign Direct Investment in Latin America. An Empirical Analysis with a Case Study on Mexico. 2005.

Bd./Vol.16   Derk Bienen: Die politische Ökonomie von Arbeitsmarktreformen in Argentinien. 2005.

Bd./Vol.17   Dierk Herzer: Exportdiversifizierung und Wirtschaftswachstum. Das Fallbeispiel Chile. 2006.

Bd./Vol.18   Jann Lay: Poverty and Distributional Impact of Economic Policies and External Shocks. Three Case Studies from Latin America Combining Macro and Micro Approaches. 2007.

Bd./Vol.19   Kenneth Harttgen: Empirical Analysis of Determinants, Distribution and Dynamics of Poverty. 2007.

Bd./Vol. 20   Stephan Klasen / Felicitas Nowak-Lehmann: Poverty, Inequality and Migration in Latin America. 2008.

Bd./Vol. 21   Isabel Günther: Empirical Analysis of Poverty Dynamics. With Case Studies from Sub-Saharan Africa. 2007.

Bd./Vol. 22   Peter Dung: Malaysia und Indonesien: Wirtschaftliche Entwicklungsstrategien in zwei Vielvölkerstaaten. 2008.

Bd./Vol. 23   Thomas Otter: Poverty, Income Growth and Inequality in Paraguay During the 1990s. Spatial Aspects, Growth Determinants and Inequality Decomposition. 2008.

Bd./Vol. 24   Mark Misselhorn: Measurement of Poverty, Undernutrition and Child Mortality. 2008.

www.peterlang.de